COLOR play

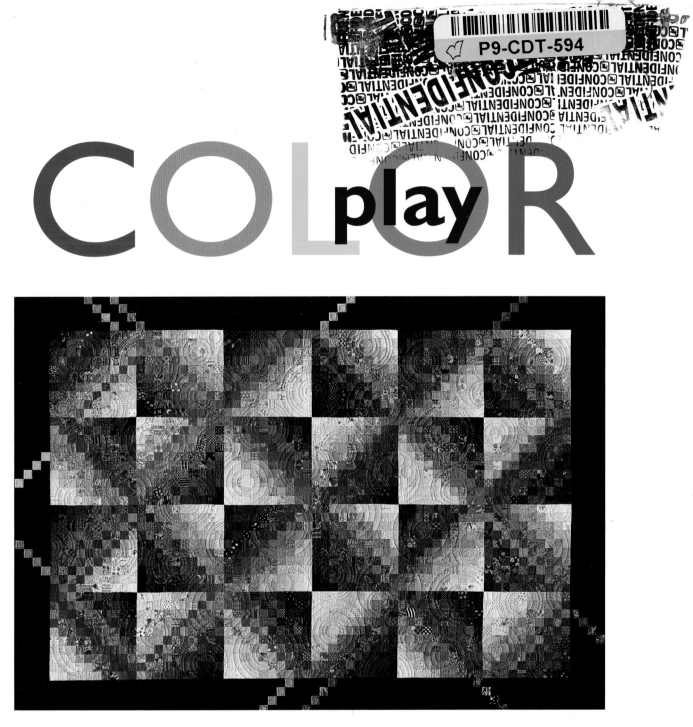

Easy Steps to Imaginative Color in Quilts

JOEN WOLFROM

Margo,
May your quilts
be filled with
joyful colors!
Joen Wolfrom

C&T PUBLISHING

Front Cover: *Nine-Patch Gone Uptown* (detail) by Kit Willey and
          Flying Free (detail) by Caryl Fallert.

Editor: Liz Aneloski
Technical Editor: Carolyn Aune
Copy Editor: Steve Cook
Production Coordinator: Diane Pedersen
Book Designer/Design Director: Aliza Kahn
Cover Designer: Aliza Kahn
Production Assistant: Kirstie L. McCormick
Nature Photographer: Joen Wolfrom
Computer Illustrators: Joen Wolfrom and Kandy Petersen
The color swatch illustrations were created in acrylic paint and then converted
to a CMYK color system on the computer. Macromedia Freehand 8.0 Software
was used for computer illustrations.
Fabric Illustrations: Joen Wolfrom

Published by C&T Publishing, Inc. P.O. Box 1456, Lafayette, California 94549

Attention Teachers:
C&T Publishing, Inc. encourages you to use this book as a text for teaching.
Contact us at 800-284-1114 or www.ctpub.com for more information about the
C&T Teachers Program.

Library of Congress Cataloging-in-Publication Data

Wolfrom, Joen.
  Color play : easy steps to imaginative color in quilts / Joen Wolfrom.

      p. cm.
  Includes bibliographical references and index.
  ISBN 1-57120-105-X (paper trade)
  1. Quilting. 2. Color in textile crafts. I. Title.
TT835.W6438 2000
746.46--dc21

                    00-008994

Printed in China
10 9 8 7

Title page:
BLACK & WHITE & EVERYTHING ELSE,
1997, 70" x 99",
Gayle P. Ropp, Vienna, Virginia

Gayle's colorful, illusionary charm quilt
uses diagonal value changes to create
luminosity, luster, and transparency. This
quilt was inspired by ideas from *More
Strip-Pieced Watercolor Magic* by Deanna
Spingola and Sally Schneider.
(Photo: Ken Wagner)

CONTENTS

Acknowledgments 4
Dedication 5
Foreword 6

Chapter One: Mother Nature and
Her Imaginative Color Play 8

Chapter Two: Mother Nature Knows Best:
The Most Beautiful Ways
to Put Colors Together 22

Chapter Three: Yummy Yellows:
Yellow, Golden-Yellow,
and Chartreuse 36

Chapter Four: Gorgeous Greens:
Green, Yellow-Green, Spring Green,
Blue-Green, and Aqua Green 48

An Exhibit Of Colorful Quilts 64

Chapter Five: Blissful Blues:
Blue, Cerulean Blue,
Turquoise, and Aqua Blue 77

Chapter Six: Very Royal Violets:
Violet, Blue-Violet, Red-Violet,
Purple, and Fuchsia 91

Chapter Seven: Rambunctious Reds:
Red, Orange-Red, Blue-Red,
and Magenta 106

Chapter Eight: Outrageous Oranges:
Orange, Yellow-Orange,
and Orange-Yellow 120

Chapter Nine: Irresistible Illusions:
Depth, Luminosity, Luster, Shadows,
Highlights, and Transparency 132

Bibliography 142
Index 142
About the Author 143

Quilt Photo Numbers Match The Page Numbers On Which They Appear.

ACKNOWLEDGMENTS

I would like to thank all who have contributed to the creation of *Color Play*. Special thanks go to Liz Aneloski, editor, for her patience and suggestions; Carolyn Aune, technical editor, for her skillful attention to technical details; Kandy Petersen, co-illustrator, for her talent and willingness to play; and Ken Wagner, product photographer, for his unbelievable ability to photograph quilts. I also wish to thank all quilters and textile artists who generously shared their work with you and me.

Joen

4A

4B

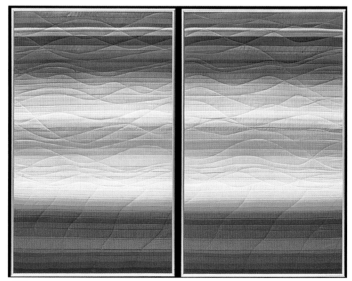

4C

5A

DEDICATION

To my brother,
Bruce Barger,

Whose unfinished symphony
Lies quietly in wait.

Although he had every intention
To celebrate the Millenium
with the rest of us,
It was not to be.

May Bruce's music
Be enjoyed and played
Forever.

5B

FOREWORD

In Search of Playful Colors

It is with great excitement that I present to you the book *Color Play—Easy Steps to Imaginative Color in Quilts*.

Many years ago, I was surprised to discover that nature was a wonderful color reference for creating quilt designs. In 1992 my first color book, *The Magical Effects of Color*, introduced many of nature's color concepts. Its immense popularity proved to me that others were as curious about color as I was. After teaching scores of color workshops during the last two decades, I have come to the conclusion that an easier, more visually powerful color book, focusing on quilters' most vexing color issues, would be very desirable and a well-used possession. Thus ideas for *Color Play* began evolving in my mind. My mission was to present simple, yet fascinating color concepts with easy instructions and tantalizing colors. In order to accomplish this goal *Color Play* has been divided into three major areas:

Color Play's first two chapters present the necessary color concepts we need to know in order to create beautiful quilts. There you can learn how colors are grouped naturally, how colors work together in the most beautiful ways, and how you can create great designs through changes in intensity, value, and temperature.

Color Play's second major color section is presented in the next six chapters. Twenty-four of the world's most beautiful colors are featured, along with some of their loveliest color companions. Nature photos, computer-made block patterns, paint-chip illustrations, and fabric illustrations are assembled to introduce these colors and present them in some of their greatest color combinations. As well, dozens of stunningly beautiful quilts help illustrate the magnificent diversity of these colors.

Color Play's last major presentation is the dessert. This final chapter features some of the most irresistible illusions. You, too, will be able to create depth, luminosity, luster, shadows, highlights, and transparency by following the guidelines introduced. Many quilts using color illusions are exhibited throughout this book.

I hope you will find *Color Play* to be a beautiful color reference that entices, stimulates, clarifies, and informs. Have fun playing with color in both simple and extraordinary ways. Enjoy!

Joen

6

7A WHISPERING STREAM,
1996, 73" × 88"
Junko Sawada, Yokohama-shi, Japan

Junko's favorite motif, the lily, is
beautifully skewed and colored to
create three-dimensionality and luster.
(Photo: Koo Saito/Studio Deep)

7B SUMMER SUNSET AT
CRESCENT BEACH,
1995, 50" × 36"
Helen Courtice, Penticton,
British Columbia, Canada

A beautiful sunset scene exhibits the
illusions of luminosity and luster.
(Photo: Courtesy of the artist)

chapter one

MOTHER NATURE & HER IMAGINATIVE

COLOR PLAY

Selecting colors for your quilt's design should be one of the most exciting and interesting phases in your quiltmaking. Hopefully, your quilt will elicit the feelings and ideas you dreamed it to have. There should be no surprises with the way the colors played together. If all went as planned, you should be ecstatic over your quilt's beauty or dynamics. The myriad of colorful ideas in *Color Play*'s pages will help you broaden your color experience and stretch your colorful imagination, ensuring that your quilts will live up to their visual potential. If you are confident about your color selection but want to create quilts with exciting visual illusions, wander through Chapter Nine for scores of illusionary ideas.

USING NATURE AS YOUR GUIDE

Years ago, as I struggled to figure out how to use color in my quilts, I began to look at nature. Slowly I realized how beautifully nature puts colors together. Nature contains a wealth of color wisdom, and I was intrigued by these natural colorations. Before long I made some interesting observations about my natural surroundings. First, I was surprised to learn the earth's colors subtly change from one season to the next. Winter grasses are a slightly different hue from spring or summer grasses. Winter sunsets differ in their intensity and hues from summer sunsets. Generally, winter flowers are more subdued than summer flowers in both blossoms and leaves. These seasonal changes made me realize I would have to use my colors differently to evoke a feeling of one particular season or another.

I further noticed that nature routinely uses several color combinations. Flowers tend to have monochromatic, analogous, and complementary color schemes. While some combinations are subtle and others quite dramatic, each is beautiful. Leaves are more apt to use a monochromatic or analogous color scheme.

Analogous, split-complementary, and complementary color schemes are often displayed in sunsets and sunrises. The ocean, lakes, and other bodies of water appear monochromatic or analogous, unless a sunrise's or sunset's hues intermingle with them.

I began to see the subtle color changes in shadows and highlights and became aware of how nature uses color in both luminosity and luster. I found myself passionately excited about the fantastic possibilities of creative color play. I became more aware of how emotions, energy, and personality are highly affected by color.

SEASONAL COLORS AND THEIR IMPORTANCE

Every color you see in the world can be separated into four main color groups. These groups are called *color scales*. Color scales simply allow us to separate colors into meaningful categories. If you want your quilt to evoke the feelings created by a particular season, time of day, or mood, simply work in the relevant color scale. If you want to incorporate illusions into your designs, it is necessary to work with one or more of these scales. The four color scales are described in this chapter: pure, tints, shades, and tones.

Pure Colors— The Dynamic Hues of Summer

The dynamic colors of summer are beautifully represented by the pure colors. Pure colors are the most intense, undiluted hues in the world. These colors are physically pure. Unlike colors in the other three groups, nothing has been added to their makeup to dilute their intense purity. The pure color hues create excitement and energy. They attract more attention than all other colors. They are often the dominant colors in dramatic art. Pure colors are brilliant and clear. Pure colors are the hues of summer. If you want to create a quilt that is summery, in imagery or emotional appeal, use the pure colors as your dominant scale (photo).

Dynamic Pure Color

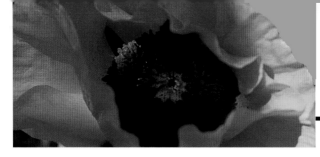

The Ives Color Wheel

Most of us learned that the *primary colors* are yellow, red, and blue. A color wheel using these three primary colors results in blends not nearly as beautiful or dynamic as the yellow-magenta-turquoise (cyan) combination used in the Ives Color Wheel. This book uses the Ives Color Wheel, since it is the specific color wheel used in fabric dyeing, print-making, and photography. (This color wheel is named for Herbert Ives, an important figure in the scientific studies of photography.) As you can see, magenta, yellow, and turquoise create the most powerfully beautiful colors in the world (page 11).

Pure colors lying halfway between the three primary colors are called *secondary colors* (page 11). These hues are orange, violet, and green. All other pure colors, which lie between the primary and secondary colors on the color wheel, are called *intermediate* or *tertiary colors* (page 11).

A quilt made primarily from the powerful pure color scale will attract immediate attention. In a show or exhibition, this quilt stands out. If you want to show energy or spirit in your design, use many pure colors. Pure-colored fabrics can be seen below. Dynamic quilts that use pure colors as their dominant scale can be seen in quilt photos 68C, 73A, and 76C.

Pure-Scale Fabrics

Many places in our homes give us great opportunities to use the energetic pure colors in our quilts. A strongly colored quilt provides a focal point in a living room, dining room, or family room. A stairwell may be another great place for a powerfully colored quilt.

Intense colors tire our eyes easily, especially when these colors are in close proximity. A baby lying on a pure-color quilt will be highly affected, as the strong colors are so close. An active child will be stimulated by strong, pure colors. Therefore, if you wish to quiet or subdue a child's behavior, use pure colors sparsely, if at all. Pure colors are much too exciting for many people to live with for hours at a time. For them, it may be better to use pure colors as accents. However, if you have a room that needs brightening, you may wish to use pure colors as your dominant scale.

The Pure Colors and Their Families

Each pure color on the color wheel is the parent of dozens of closely related hues in its own family. Thus, every pure color is the head of its own color family. The pure color may be referred to as the root or parent color of these offspring hues. Besides the pure hue, each family consists of the hues from the tint, shade, and tone scales. Each scale has its own requirements and personality. Also, each scale is closely related to one of the earth's seasons.

Tints—The Fragile Hues of Spring

As the earth awakens from its winter sleep, soft colors begin to emerge gently before our eyes. These delicate colors are called tints. The tint scale includes all colors between white and the pure color. Although there are some pure-colored flowers, such as the yellow jonquil, that appear in spring, the hues of spring mainly come from the gentle, soft tint scale. They are often referred to as pastels. Examples of tints are soft yellow, celery green, mint green, powder blue, robin's egg blue, coral, lavender, pink, peach, apricot, and cream.

Tint Scale

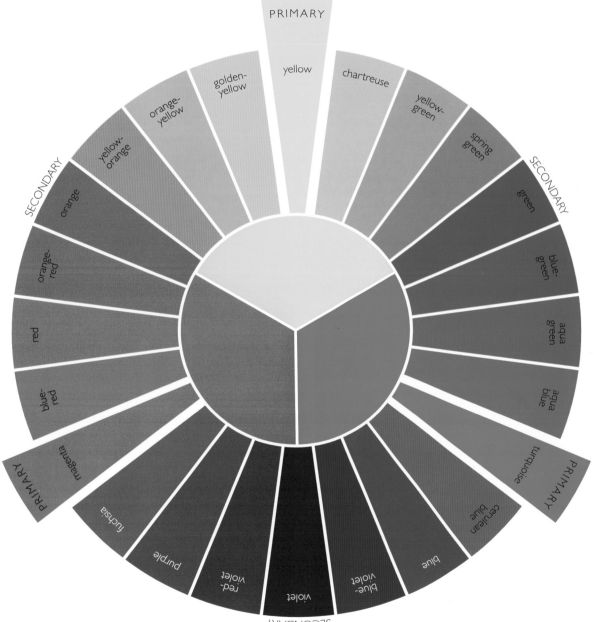

PRIMARY

yellow
chartreuse
golden-yellow
yellow-green
orange-yellow
spring green
yellow-orange
SECONDARY
green
SECONDARY
blue-green
orange
aqua green
orange-red
aqua blue
red
turquoise
blue-red
PRIMARY
magenta
cerulean blue
PRIMARY
fuchsia
blue
purple
blue-violet
red-violet
violet
SECONDARY

Ives Color Wheel

Tints are created by combining a pure color with white. All tints are lighter than their pure color. Most tints are delicate and fragile.

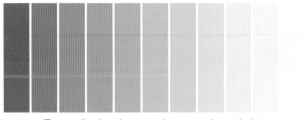

Tints—all colors between the pure color and white

Below, a twenty-four-step pastel color wheel shows one tint from each hue. Obviously there are dozens more tints than we see here, as each color family has many tints within its tint scale. You can see many more tint hues in your favorite color's chapter. Since every tint has white in its makeup, white is the best neutral hue for tints.

Color Wheel with Tints

If you use mostly tints in your quilt, your design may have a feeling of spring, rebirth, or freshness. Also, having tints as your dominant scale may give your quilt a sense of the soft fragility often seen in spring flowers.

Tint-Scale Fabrics

A light color, such as yellow, has few tints, because it does not take very many steps to move from white to the pure color. The yellow tint scale includes all colors from blush white (white with a hint of light yellow) to almost pure yellow.

Yellow Tints—from pure yellow to blush white

A dark color, such as violet, has many tints, because it takes a lot of steps to move from white to the pure color violet. Violet's tint scale moves from blush white (white with a hint of lavender) to almost pure violet.

Violet Tints—from pure violet to blush white

Although it's not as vibrant a color group as the shade or pure scales, the tint scale is remarkably beautiful. Be sure to take advantage of the tints in your favorite color's family. It is difficult to observe their beauty from a distance because of the delicacy of their hues. Quilts created mainly from the tint scale can be seen in photos 5A and 67B.

The Dual Personality of Shades

Adding black to a pure color creates a shade. Therefore, any blackened color is part of the shade scale. If only a small amount of black is added, the pure color is minimally changed. The more black that is added, the darker the color becomes. Blackened blue becomes navy blue. If this blue appears nearly black, it's called ink navy.

Blue Shades—from pure blue to ink navy

A slightly blackened red becomes a reddish rust. As black is added, the colors become varying hues of rich brown. The best neutral for shades is black, because all shades have black in their makeup. Shades have two pronounced personalities: warm and cool.

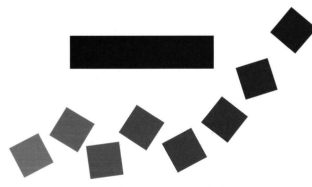

Red Shades—from pure red to rich, dark brown

Warm Shades and Their Brilliant Autumn Imagery

In nature, the powerful pure colors of summer change subtly as autumn arrives. Due to cold night temperatures and rainfall, nature's colors begin to blacken. The result is the much anticipated display of autumn colors in our deciduous landscape.

These shaded warm colors change considerably from their pure roots. Blackened chartreuse, yellow, and golden-yellow, create a wide variety of olive greens.

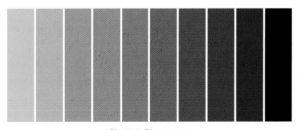

Shaded Chartreuse

Shaded Yellow

Shaded Golden-Yellow

Shaded Orange-Yellow

Blackened orange-yellow, yellow-orange and orange create different degrees of khakis, rusts, and browns

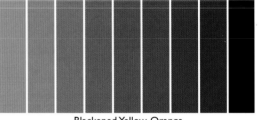

Blackened Yellow-Orange

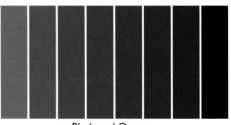

Blackened Orange

If you want to create an autumn quilt, use the beautiful warm shaded hues. You can see a sample of these fabrics below. Photos 72A and 72B show a few beautiful quilts in which the warm shade scale is dominant.

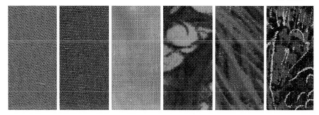

Warm Shade-Scale—Autumn Colors

Cool Shades and Their Darkened Imagery

Shaded cool colors give us imagery of such things as night scenes and dark forests. Their shaded personalities are similar to their pure root, but darker.

Cool Shades

Winter-toned hues

Often *dark* or *deep* precede the cool shade names: dark blue, dark blue-violet, dark violet, and deep violet. Other shaded cool hues include jade green, indigo blue, ultramarine blue, royal blue, teal blue, and navy. A fabric selection of cool shades can be seen below. The quilt photo 34B uses cool shades.

Cool Shade-Scale Fabrics   Cool Shades

Tones—The Subtle Hues of Winter

As temperatures decline further, the earth turns from rich autumn shades to subtle, quiet hues. Most flowers disappear from the landscape. Leaves have fallen, leaving the deciduous branches bare. A hush seems to fall over the land as the earth's landscape begins its winter sleep. As winter deepens, the colors are subdued by an overlying grayness. The fabric selection below shows toned fabrics for wintry effects. Quilts that elicit this quiet, wintry effect can be seen in photos 65A and 131C.

Any color that has a grayed, wintry, subdued, or veiled quality is from the tone scale. Nature provides many examples of toned hues. They are beautiful, quiet, and calming. We are surrounded with peaceful toned hues in mist, fog, rainstorms, and during the coolness of dawn. Tones are wonderful to use in a design when you want to create a subtle effect. Toned quilts are perfect for bedrooms, where sleep and respite are the focus. They also are great to use for small children's quilts, since tones do not usually cause visual stimulation.

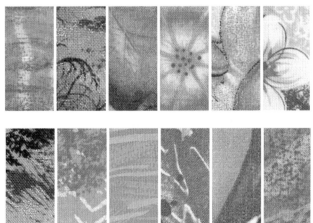

Toned Fabrics for Wintry Effects

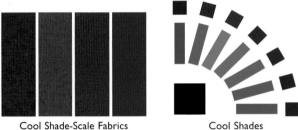

Calming Tone Scale

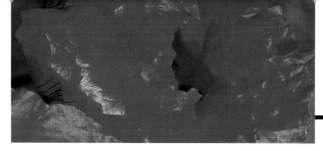

There are more colors in the tone scale than in any other scale because every pure color, tint, and shade can be grayed or toned. Aqua green and fuchsia can be seen below as they change from their pure, tint, and shaded forms to toned hues. Since all tones are grayed, the best neutral to use with tones is gray.

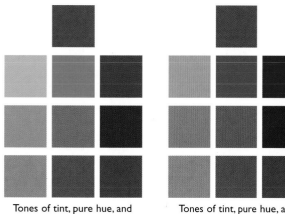

Tones of tint, pure hue, and shade of aqua green

Tones of tint, pure hue, and shade of fuschia

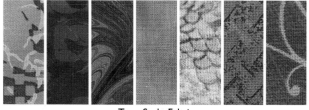

Tone-Scale Fabrics

A selection of toned fabrics is shown above. Photos 65A, 65B, 130A, 130C, and 130D show quilts made primarily from the subtle tones.

FEELING A COLOR'S INTENSITY

All pure colors are intense because nothing dilutes their purity (see color wheel on page 11). Whenever a pure color is diluted, its intensity lessens. A color can be diluted when white or black is added. Also, a color is less intense when it has been grayed or toned. The apricot rose (whitened), the dark red leaves (blackened), and the hydrangea petals (grayed) show little intensity. They lack the visual strength and drama of the pure, intense hues.

Whitened, blackened, and greyed images lack intensity.

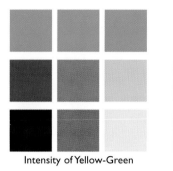

Intensity of Yellow-Green   Intensity of Red

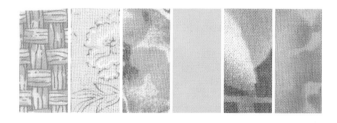

The Reef
High-Valued Design
No Value Contrast

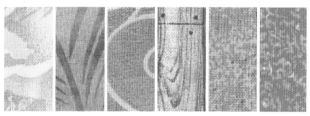

High-Value Colored Fabrics

Photos 21 and 71D show intensely colored quilts. Those showing little color intensity include quilts in photos 131A, 131B, and 131C.

THE VALUE OF COLOR

For most of us, the darkness or lightness of art, rather than its subject matter, determines our reaction to it. We are so sensitive to light that it affects our personality and emotions. Choosing how light or dark a design will be is every bit as important as choosing colors. In design, the word *value* is used to describe the lightness or darkness of a color.

High-Valued Hues

Colors close to white are called high in value or high valued. They usually seem light, airy, or delicate.

High-Valued Colors

If you enjoy the soft, gentle high-value colors, incorporate a few middle-valued colors too. Otherwise, your design will fade out and be difficult to see. This disappointing design flaw can be seen in the block The Reef, above right. Fabrics high in value can be seen at right. A high-valued quilt can be seen in photo 6.

Low-Valued Hues

Colors close to black are low in value or low valued. They incorporate deep, rich, dark colors.

Low-Valued Colors

If you love to work with the deep, dark, low-valued hues, include a few middle-valued colors too. If all of your colors are dark, the design disappears or is difficult to discern. This value problem is shown in The Reef on the following page. A selection of low-valued fabrics can also be seen on the following page. Quilts made from low-valued hues can be seen in photos 34B, 68A, and 141A.

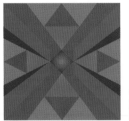

The Reef
Low-Valued Design
No Value Contrast

The Reef
Middle-Valued Design
No Value Contrast

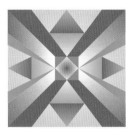

The Reef
Middle-Valued Design
Good Value Contrast

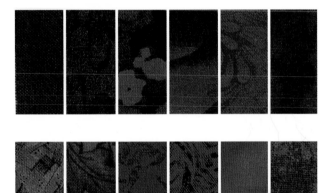

Low-Valued Colored Fabrics

Beautiful Value Play

When value contrast is present, a design is much more likely to live up to its desired potential (see photos 64C, 65C, 66B, 70B, and 75A). The Reef pattern looks dynamic when value contrast is present (above, right).

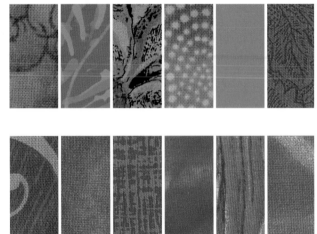

Middle-Value Colored Fabrics

Middle-Valued Hues

Those hues neither close to black nor white are middle-valued colors. If you enjoy working with middle values, be sure to add some value contrast. The middle-valued design in the next column shows little value contrast, so the design disappears before our eyes. So, use enough value contrast or variation to enhance your design. Middle-valued fabrics can be seen at the right. A quilt created mostly in middle-valued fabrics can be seen in photo 65B.

Middle-Valued Colors

Colors appear to change their values in relation to other hues. This illusion seems extraordinary when we watch color values appear to shift in a design. To illustrate this phenomenon, the narrow strips of middle-value deep pink and middle-valued gray appear to change as they move from the high-valued hues to the low-valued hues. Amazingly each strip is the same color from left to right (page 19).

Wide Value Range

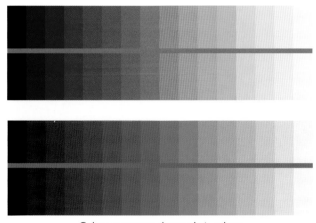

Colors appear to change their values
in relation to other hues.

Nature gives us many opportunities to study value. If you love drama, working with strong contrasts may be your favorite way to work with value. These value extremes can be quite stunning in a design (see photos 64C, 65C, 66B, and 75A).

Limited Value Range

A limited value range can create a calm mood or subtle design (see photo 65B).

You can also move from the very lightest to the very darkest values throughout the entire design. Using the entire value spectrum creates a beautiful, rich effect (see photos 7A, 65A, 66C, 69A, 69B, and 74A).

Total Value Spectrum

If your design has little value change, strengthen it with another design focus, such as texture (see photo below). As you experiment with value, learn to recognize the value style you innately prefer.

Limited value spectrum is strengthened through textural interest.

CHANGING A COLOR'S TEMPERATURE

Warm Colors

Cool Colors

Colors can suggest feelings of warmth or coolness. Warm colors are associated with sunlight, heat, excitement, and happiness. They have more ability to be luminous than cool colors do. Cool colors are associated with relaxation, mist, night, shadows, and refreshing coolness. Warm colors advance visually while cool colors tend to recede into the distance (see photos 4A, 7A, 71B, and 76A).

Manipulating adjacent hues can make any color register as either cool or warm.

Colors are fluid and ever-changing in their effect, depending on their placement and the surrounding colors. If you want warm hues in your art to appear even warmer, place them next to obviously cool colors. If you want to accentuate cool colors, place them next to warm colors. You can make each appear warmer or cooler by using temperature extremes (see photos 68A, 68C, and 141A). Nature does this exceptionally well with her sunrises and sunsets. Make it a habit to watch these daily interplays between warm and cool colors in nature. Then use them as your color inspiration for future design.

Blue-red appears warm when teamed with blue-violet.

When blue-red is paired with orange-red, the former hue presents a cool personality.

A teal appears cool next to warm green, but appears warm next to cerulean blue.

PUTTING IT ALL TOGETHER

If we study nature well, we will observe ways to help us make important color decisions. Here are a few guidelines to remember:

Select one color scale (pure, tint, shade, or tone) to be visually dominant in your design. You may include all four scales in your design, but one scale should be more influential or more pronounced than the others. Also, determine which value (high, medium, or low) will be dominant. Include value change in your design. It can be subtle, strong, limited, or full ranged.

Now for the big decision: selecting the colors for your design. Always select a color you really like for your design's major feature. After you have chosen this color, decide on your companion colors. To help you in this matter, Chapter Two is filled with information and many ideas based on nature and its most popular color schemes. These ideas will allow you to take many colorful journeys in your own design play.

Chapters Three through Eight are dedicated to twenty-four of our most beautiful colors, their characteristics, and color combinations that make them look stunning in a design. Select your feature color and then go to the chapter that highlights it.

Chapter Nine is dedicated to color illusions. Those featured are depth, luminosity, luster, shadows, highlights, and transparency. If you want to add any of these illusions to your design, refer to this chapter.

Have a great time selecting colors for your next project and experimenting with a few glorious illusions. Most of all . . . have fun playing with color!

21 AUTUMN ALTERNATIVES I,
1999, 57" × 42"
Bonny Tinling, Vista, California

The use of both clear, yellow-toned colors and deep, rich shades amongst middle-valued hues creates highlights and shadows in this lively design.
(Photo: Courtesy of the artist)

chapter two
MOTHER NATURE KNOWS BEST

the most beautiful ways to put colors together

Through the ages, artists have carefully observed nature's blending of hues, noting that the natural play of color leads to beautiful outcomes. Nature's choices range from the subtlest combinations to the most dramatic. In this chapter you are presented with descriptions and illustrations of nature's most beloved, well-used, and beautiful color schemes. Also, colorful hints and suggestions are included. After reading about these color schemes, go directly to your favorite color's chapter. There you will find different plans for each color. After you have perused your color's chapter, decide which color scheme you would like to use in your upcoming project.

The five most popular color schemes are all beautiful, but they reflect different styles and outcomes. Select the one that works best with your design—or the one that excites you most. These color schemes are guidelines rather than restrictive rules. Your unique ideas, emotions, and creative needs should take precedence over generalized rules. Have a color wheel nearby so you can see the color relationships easily. See the color wheels on pages 11 and 24.

THE SOPHISTICATED MONOCHROMATIC COLOR SCHEME

Monochromatic Color Scheme

In a *monochromatic* color scheme, the colors in the design all come from the same color family. Nature contains scores of examples of monochromatic color schemes. The subtle changes of desert sand can be beautifully monochromatic. A cold, bleak winter day can display hues from one family alone. The monochromatic scheme can be sophisticated and elegant. The most important ingredient in this color scheme is value—the contrast of light and dark hues. This contrast can be subtle, softly contrasted, or strongly apparent.

When working, keep in mind that a design is far more striking or interesting when value or intensity changes are present. For instance, if you want to create a purple design, you can use pure purple and any of its tint, shade, or tone scales to create good value contrast.

Purple Tint Scale

Purple Shade Scale

Purple Tone Scale

Besides value, you may wish to work with intensity by moving hues from the most intense pure color to its most toned hues. An example from nature shows a flower's color moves from a beautiful blue-red to a slightly grayed, dusty pink.

Intensity: The color moves from blue-red to dusty pink.

The monochromatic color scheme is the most difficult plan to work in, because the fabrics must strictly adhere to the monochromatic coloring guidelines. Unfortunately, most of us do not have fabrics with a broad value spectrum of one color family readily available. Therefore, you may have to spend many months acquiring a good selection of hues from one color family before beginning a monochromatic design.

Do not merge neighboring color wheel hues. For instance, fuchsia or red-violet hues cannot be added to purple's monochromatic color scheme.

Use only one color family for a monochromatic color scheme

Do not use neighboring colors for a monochromatic color scheme.

The pattern Celebration uses the monochromatic color scheme with magenta. The entire design is created through value changes. A monochromatic quilt setting of Celebration is shown on page 32.

Celebration
Monochromatic

A MARRIAGE OF COLORS—THE COMPLEMENTARY PARTNERS

Colors that lie opposite each other on the color wheel are especially beautiful together. They complement each other extraordinarily well. See color wheel on page 11 also.

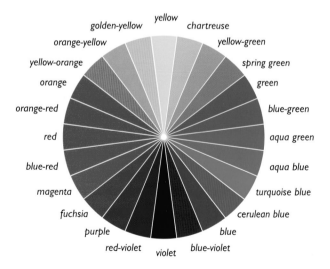

When these two opposing colors are used together, it is called a *complementary* color scheme. Nature uses this plan often in its coloring. Sometimes this is dramatic; at other times nature's complementary use is so subtle it can be almost overlooked.

Subtle Complementary Color Schemes

Complementary colors are beautiful when a variety of scales are used (pure color, tints, shades, tones).

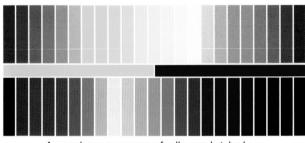

A complementary range of yellow and violet hues.

You can use additional hues if you blend the two opposing colors together. These intermingled and blended hues are found by painting one pure complementary color into the other.

Intermingled and Blended Yellow and Violet

Finding a Color's Complementary Color

If you want to work with a complementary color scheme, it is important that you have the exact complement of your selected color. Do not guess. If you combine two colors that are not quite opposites, the result is disappointing. When you combine true complements, the results can be stunning.

Often we read that blue and orange are complements. However, if you look at orange and blue and their positions on the color wheel below, you can see they do not lie exactly opposite each other.

Orange and Blue	Orange and Turquoise	Orange-yellow and Blue

Orange's complement is actually turquoise (cyan) and blue's complement is orange-yellow. A selection of hues from the turquoise-orange complement can be seen below.

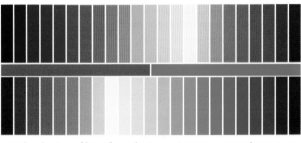

A selection of hues from the turquoise-orange complement.

Also, purple is often mistakenly substituted for violet. Violet lies opposite yellow, whereas purple lies opposite yellow-green.

Although purple and yellow may be in a design together, they shouldn't be used as complements. They are stunning with their own partners, but somewhat jarring when mismatched.

Complements, Purple and Yellow-Green, Violet and Yellow

Finding the Afterimage

You can find your color's exact partner by finding its afterimage. An afterimage is a tint from your selected color's complement. You can use an easy, quick method to find the afterimage. All you need is good light, a large, white piece of paper, and your selected color.

Begin by placing a swatch of your selected color on a large piece of white paper (use fabric, paper, or a paint chip for your color swatch). Stare at the color swatch for approximately 30 seconds. Soon a light hue will begin glowing around the swatch's edges. It may even move around. After staring at it a short time, slide your swatch away while you continue to stare at that spot on the paper. Try not to blink while you do this. The afterimage (the glowing color) will appear for a few fleeting seconds. This afterimage color will always be light, as it is the tint of your swatch's complementary color. It's an amazing phenomenon. You might practice finding afterimages of several colors you enjoy. The illustration below shows four different blues with their complementary colors and afterimages. Note: If you wear glasses, you may wish to take your glasses off for this exercise, since many glasses have a coating that diminishes this experiment.

Once you have detected your color's afterimage, find its tint scale in one of the following chapters. After matching the afterimage with its tint-scale, you can see its pure hue and many other hues within that color family. Use any hues from this complement's family in your complementary design.

Using Complementary Colors

As you plan your design, remember that one complementary color family should be visually dominant. You should not allow both colors to have equal visual power, as this creates visual competition between colors, and then the design can suffer. When there is no dominant color, the viewers' eyes jump from one spot to another, not knowing where to rest. It causes an uncomfortable feeling.

To create a complementary design, use fabrics from both color families. Do not use a fabric that includes an unrelated color. Selections of fabrics for complementary color schemes can be seen on pages 38, 50, 84, 99, 108, 113, and 127.

Each color's chapter shows a selection of complementary partners' hues. Use these illustrations as a guide. The block Celebration is shown here and on page 32 in a complementary color scheme.

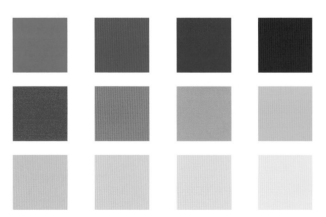

Four different blues with their complementary
colors and afterimages.

Celebration
Complementary

BEAUTIFUL COLOR HARMONY WITH ANALOGOUS COLORS

Nature often uses closely related colors to create beautiful visual harmony. This natural harmony is very appealing and may be the reason why this is the most popular color scheme among quilters. We call a color plan *analogous* whenever colors lying side by side on the color wheel are used in a design. Many exquisite colorings in nature grandly illustrate the beauty of this harmonic color plan. Keep your camera handy for these awesome color displays. They are great references to use in your own designs.

Analogous Color Schemes

Guidelines for Analogous Colorings

Use the color wheel on page 11 to help you decide what colors you will use in your design. For best results, use three, five, or seven analogous colors. Make certain the color range is less than one-third of the color wheel.

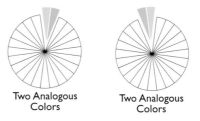

Two Analogous Colors   Two Analogous Colors

Designs using only two analogous colors are less beautiful than those with a wider range. Two-color designs are enhanced if one more neighboring color is added—even if it's only in small amounts. If you prefer subtlety, use three colors. If you wish more interest or drama, use five or seven analogous colors.

Three Analogous Colors   Five Analogous Colors   Seven Analogous Colors

In an analogous color scheme, quilters can vary color values and intensities. The hues used can span from the lightest tints to the darkest shades.

The selected color may be positioned on either end of the analogous color range. This allows you two more analogous color options (see below).

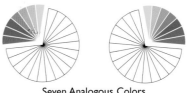

Seven Analogous Colors
with Yellow at One End

A range of analogous hues is shown below. Here orange-yellow, golden-yellow, yellow, chartreuse, and yellow-green families are joined in an analogous partnership. Any or all of these hues may be used in a design. You will find a detailed view of your selected color's analogous partners in its chapter.

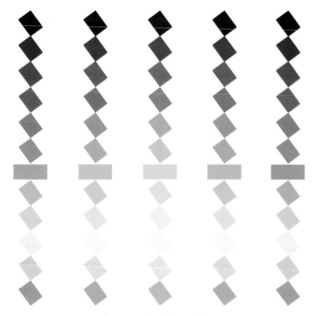

A range of analogous hues

You can see fabric selections for analogous color schemes on pages 41, 44, 55, 58, 79, 87, 102, 116, and 124. Fabric manufacturers often feature analogously-colored fabrics.

The pattern Celebration is shown in a five-hue analogous coloring on page 32. Quilts using analogous color schemes can be seen in photos 64B, 64C, 72A, and 76D.

Celebration
Analogous

THE SPLIT-COMPLEMENTARY COLOR SCHEME—ADDING A TEMPERATURE SHIFT

If you are looking for a color bargain worth its weight in gold, you will love working with the split-complementary color scheme. It combines the analogous and complementary color plans. This color scheme appeals because of its natural temperature change, which is a wonderful design enhancement. In nature this color scheme is seen most often in sunrises and sunsets. For instance, the sky is often painted with a sunset of yellow and violet along with neighboring analogous hues of one of the complementary partners.

In a split-complementary plan, the complement (the temperature-shifting color) always lies opposite the middle analogous color. The analogous color band is usually comprised of three or five colors. If you are working with cool analogous hues, the complement will be warm. If you are using warm analogous colors, the complementary color will be cool.

Cool analogous hues,
warm complement

Warm analogous hues,
cool complement

Magenta, purple, and violet provide the analogous range in a split-complementary color scheme. Purple, the middle analogous color, combines with its complement, yellow-green, to complete the color arrangement. You can use a selection of each color's tints, tones, and shades.

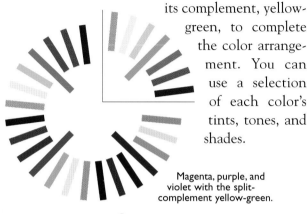

Magenta, purple, and violet with the split-complement yellow-green.

Use this color combination if you love the temperature shift a split-complementary color plan provides. Select one color family to play a dominant role and another to take a secondary position. The remaining colors should be used as accents.

Fabric selections for split-complementary color schemes are shown on pages 45, 56, 88, 103, 109, 117, 125, and 128. First, determine your quilt's analogous color range and select all fabrics that will fit within this range. Next, determine the middle analogous color. Find its complement. Then select fabrics that will be part of that color plan.

The block Celebration is shown on page 32 in a split-complementary color scheme. Photos 7A and 35B, show quilts using the split-complementary color scheme.

Celebration
Split-complementary

THE UNLIKELY TRIO—THE TRIADIC COLOR SCHEME

Sometimes three colors blend beautifully in a seemingly unrelated grouping. The beauty cannot be denied, yet, to the novice eye, the relationship seems random. Amazingly, it is not. This color trio has a very firm relationship, as the colors lie equal distances from each other on the color wheel. When a trio of these colors is combined, the color scheme is called triadic.

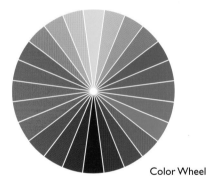

Color Wheel

Magenta, yellow, and turquoise make up the most well known triadic combination. This combination is called the primary triadic color scheme.

Primary Triadic
Color Scheme

You can use scores of hues from each color family in your design. Also, you can mix these colors to create blended hues.

The secondary colors green, violet, and orange lie halfway between the primary colors and lie equal distances from each other. The pure hues and any of their tints, shades, and tones may be used in this color scheme. You can also create beautiful blended hues by mixing these three colors together.

Secondary Triadic
Color Scheme

Choosing Your Own Triadic Partners

Find your own triadic partners by first selecting your featured color. Then find the other two colors that lie equal distances from this color. If you are using a twenty-four step color wheel, your colors will be eight steps away from each other (3 x 8 = 24; see pages 11 and 24). If you love aqua blue, count eight colors away in either direction—fuchsia and golden-yellow.

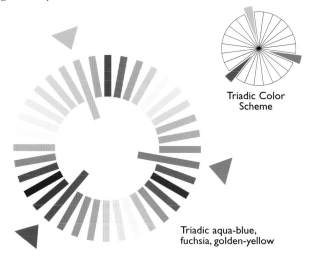

Triadic Color
Scheme

Secondary Triadic
Color Scheme

Triadic aqua-blue,
fuchsia, golden-yellow

Blended Hues

These three pure colors, their tints, shades, tones, and any blends may be used in your design.

You may use a wide assortment of hues from each of the color families in your design, or you may combine these pure hues with one another to find their blended hues.

A triadic design's success depends on good color control. Have one color family play a dominant role. This helps create unity and allows your eyes a place to rest. Use another color family as the secondary color. The third color family plays a lesser role.

This color scheme looks quite different from the other settings. Pages 51, 80, 100, and 114 show triadic selections. After determining your quilt's triadic colors, select fabrics from each color family. Do not use fabrics that incorporate hues that are not part of your color plan. If you use paints to blend the three triadic colors, you may find fabrics with these blends. If so, use these fabrics in your designs too. Photos 67D and 68C show quilts using this color scheme.

The Block Celebration in the triadic combination of magenta, yellow, and turquoise is shown here and on page 32 in a triadic quilt setting.

Celebration
Triadic

OTHER COLOR PLANS

You may wish to investigate nature further to see other ways it uses color. Observing the colors in trees, bushes, flowers, and even weeds will expand your visual knowledge.

Try to isolate as many hues as you can in the object you find. Take a picture of it if it cannot be brought into your workroom. Attempt to pull out all of the colors you observe (isolate them, if you can). Then build your design around these colors in similar proportions. In this way, you will create the same effect as your object. Then select the fabrics to match these colors. It should be beautiful!

PLAYING WITH COLOR

As quilters, few of us have had formal studies in color. That, however, should not keep us from having a great time experimenting! Each of us can start our own color journey with a little bit of information and a desire to increase our abilities. I suggest you work with the colors that most interest you. Slowly expand your repertoire by continuing to work with those familiar colors in varying color combinations.

Use this book as your own personal color resource. Simply select one of your favorite color families with which to work. Then go to that color family's section in the book. You will find enormous color-play possibilities with the various color schemes. Choose the one that will give the best visual results.

To experiment with color placement, use colored pencils, crayons, watercolor pencils, or a computer program. Color loosely—even scribble, if you wish. All you want is a visual idea as to how the colors may work with your design, so don't spend a lot of time coloring individual shapes. Your best coloring will be with fabric, so don't get too bogged down with putting color to paper. If coloring on paper frustrates you, go directly to fabric play.

Most block patterns look great no matter what color scheme is used. However, some patterns are stunning only when one specific color plan is used. Experiment with your block pattern in order to select the color scheme you think will create the most dynamic results for your chosen design and its featured color. Your future quilts can evolve into amazingly beautiful, dynamic quilts. Your color use will become second nature to you with a little experience.

BLOCK PLAY WITH COLOR SCHEMES

It is amazing to see how the color schemes can create such different design effects. Here the pattern Celebration is used with magenta in five color scheme options

Many more variations can be created by changing your hue selection, by switching the color placement, or by putting another color in the dominant position. Each chapter has a pattern selection illustrating the visual differences between major color plans. Encourage yourself to use your favorite color in all of these color schemes. Have fun playing with color!

Analogous

Monochromatic

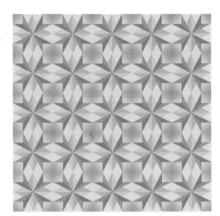

Split-
Complementary

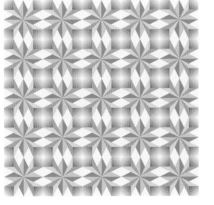

Complementary

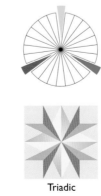
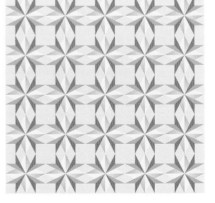

Triadic

33A CREATIVE TRACES, 1998, 43" x 52"
Joan Dyer, Redondo Beach, California

Creative Traces was pieced with irregularly shaped pieces of hand-dyed and hand-painted fabrics. The flowers were made using quilting thread.
(Photo: Ken Wagner)

33B AUTUMN MEADOWS, 1998, 49" x 38"
Anneliese M. Carl, Hamburg, New York

This quilt was inspired by the purple asters and goldenrod blooming in autumn along the country roads in western New York. This three-dimensional triangular design was inspired by a workshop with Alison Goss.
(Photo: Ken Wagner)

33C MORNING SUN, 1996, 48" x 48"
Jean Wells, Sisters, Oregon

Jean has created her own "quilt garden" by taking a flower block and expanding it. Radiating quilting lines accentuate the sunlight flowing into the garden.
(Photo: Ross Chandler)

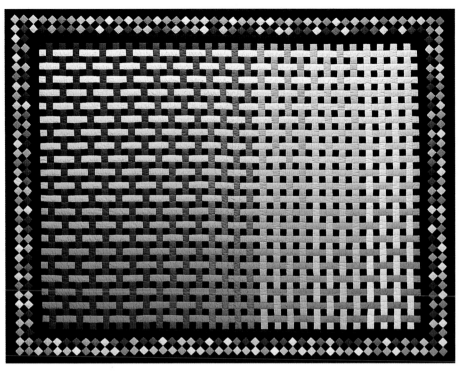

34A WEEFFOURTJE (WEAVING ERROR), 1995, 79" × 63"
lek Collet, Heemstede, Holland

Rectangular color bars and navy squares create this lustrous design. After finishing the top, lek noticed one blue color bar was missing. It looked like a weaving error; hence the name.
(Photo: Gerard Van Yperen)

34B SPRING NOTES, 1999, 62" × 59"
Carol Webb, Bend, Oregon

Transparency and luminosity seem to appear in Carol's free-flowing design. The warm analogous hues contrast with touches of cool reds.
(Photo: Courtesy of the artist)

34C FAINTING SPELL, 1995, 44" × 44"
Martha W. Ginn, Hattiesburg, Mississippi

Martha placed dark squares and dark triangles together, thus creating a natural value change. Bev Young's *Spring Garden* inspired this quilt.
(Photo: Brent Wallace)

35A SUNFLOWERS, 1996, 68" × 60"
Jean Wells, Sisters, Oregon

Jean's inspiration for this quilt was the interplay of shapes and colors between flowers and foliage. Stitch-and-flip leaves and New York Beauty-style sunflowers blend fabrics to create this original design.
(Photo: Ross Chandler)

35B YTENE—LAND OF THE JUTES,
1997, 60" × 65"
Carol Rowland, Devon, England

This autumnal quilt, uses highlights and shadows in its design. *Ytene* was inspired by workshops from Cynthia England and Joen Wolfrom.
(Photo: Dave Blunden, Ltd.)

35C AMBIGUITY I, 1998, 50" × 54"
Paul Schutte, Potchefskoom, South Africa

This wonderfully subtle quilt is created from warm autumnal shades and subtle tones. This interpretive design was made entirely from squares and triangles.
(Photo: Marius van der Westhuizen)

chapter three

YUMMY YELLOWS

yellow
golden-yellow
chartreuse

Welcome to yellow and its closely related neighbors chartreuse and golden-yellow.

These are the colors of warmth, brilliance, energy, and spirit. When we think of yellow, we visualize all sorts of favorite and nostalgic images: daffodils nodding their brilliant heads in early spring; butterflies flitting from bush to bush in summer; yummy yellow fruits and vegetables, such as lemons, grapefruit, bananas, yellow peppers, and pineapples. Spring and summer bring us a joyous array of welcoming yellow flowers, from buttercups to exquisite roses.

This chapter is broken into three color sections: yellow, golden-yellow, and chartreuse. Select the color of your choice. Then decide what color scheme you wish to work in. Go to Chapter Two for detailed instructions about your choice. If you need more information about working with color scales, values, and temperature, or other general color hints, refer to Chapter One. Have fun working with the brightest, hottest colors on the earth!

YUMMY YELLOW

Pure yellow is strong—nothing has diluted its strength. Tinted yellows can range from a blush white tinged with yellow to a yellow just slightly lighter than the pure color. When black is added to yellow, the hues change magically to various olives. These hues can be used for autumn colorings.

When gray is added to pure or shaded yellow, subtle olive hues appear. They are muted compared to the shades. When light yellow is toned, warm yellowish gray and beige are created. If you enjoy yellow, use it to create exciting designs. If you prefer subtle colorings, use yellow tones. If you love autumnal colors, use yellow's shades.

Working with Yellow in a Monochromatic Color Plan

Use only those hues that specifically belong to the yellow family when working monochromatically. A yellow monochromatic design from blush yellow to dark olive can be beautiful and vibrant.

Spinning Around the Block
Monochromatic

The hues on this page can be used monochromatically or they may be used in any other color scheme that includes yellow.

Tints (yellow + white)

Shades (yellow + black)

Tones (pure yellow + gray)

Tones (light yellow + gray)

Tones (dark yellow + gray)

Playing with Yellow and Its Complementary Partner Violet

Yellow and violet lie opposite each other on the color wheel. This partnership is very popular in nature and design, as their hues are glorious together. Spinning Around the Block is shown in a complementary color scheme on page 46. A fabric selection is shown at the right.

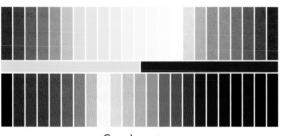

Complementary

Complementary

Spinning Around
the Block
Complementary

Complementary
Yellow and Violet

Yellow and Its Wonderfully Vibrant Analogous Neighbors

Yellow and its analogous colors create exciting designs. You can use three to seven neighboring hues with excellent results. (See quilt photo 75C.) Yellow can be positioned on the outer edges of the analogous range too. Spinning Around the Block is placed in an analogous setting on page 46.

Yellow and Its Primary Triadic Partnership

Since yellow, magenta, and turquoise are equal distances apart on the color wheel, they are the partners in this primary triadic color scheme (see quilt photo 68C). Use these three pure colors, as well as any of their tints, shades, and tones. Yellow is shown with its triadic partners in Spinning Around the Block on page 46 and Storm at Sea on page 89.

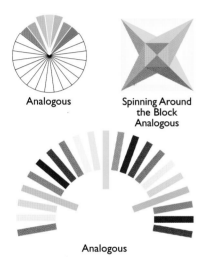

Analogous

Spinning Around
the Block
Analogous

Analogous

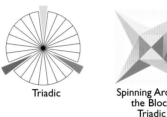

Triadic

Spinning Around
the Block
Triadic

Triadic

Playing with a Temperature Change—Split-Complementary

A split-complementary color scheme combines yellow and violet with the former color's neighboring hues. This is a great color plan to use because of the natural temperature shift between the warm analogous hues and violet. Spinning Around the Block can be seen in a split-complementary color scheme on page 46.

Split-Complementary

Spinning Around
the Block
Split-Complimentary

GLOWING GOLDEN-YELLOW —A TOUCH OF GOLD

In its pure state golden-yellow is light, luminous, and very warm. Golden-yellow has a different personality than yellow, and it 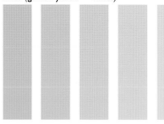 creates a different emotional feeling. The soft golden-yellow hues from the tint scale are lovely in their fragile state. Notice how dramatically golden-yellow changes to warm olive as black is added. The tones are more muted than the shades. Golden-yellow shades and darkened tones are wonderful in autumnal quilts. Golden-yellow tints become soft, yellow beige hues when toned.

Golden-Yellow Standing on Its Own—Monochromatically

If you would like to use the golden-yellow family in a monochromatic design, use pure golden-yellow along with its tints, shades, and tones.

Delectable Mountains
Monochromatic

The hues on this page can be used monochromatically or they may be used in any other color scheme that includes golden-yellow.

Tints (golden-yellow + white)

Shades (golden-yellow + black)

Tones (pure golden-yellow + gray)

Tones (light golden-yellow + gray)

Tones (dark golden-yellow + gray)

Golden-Yellow and Its Complementary Partner Blue-Violet

Golden-yellow is lovely in conjunction with its complement blue-violet. Often we see this combination in sunsets and sunrises. Pages 47 and 104 show the patterns Delectable Mountains and Dutch Mill created in complementary color schemes.

Delectable Mountains
Complementary

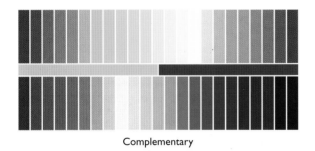

Complementary

Complementary

Golden-Yellow and Its Analogous Opportunities

If you love working with hot colors, consider using golden-yellow in an analogous plan. This color plan occurs frequently in nature. Use three, five, or seven analogous hues to create an exciting design with golden-yellow as the middle color. You can position golden-yellow on either end of your analogous range too. A selection of fabrics for this color combination can be seen at the right. Delectable Mountains is shown in an analogous color plan on page 47.

Delectable Mountains
Analogous

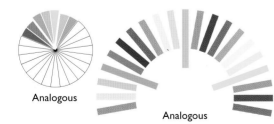

Analogous

Analogous

Analogous
Golden-Yellow

Golden-Yellow and Its Split-Complementary Options

Golden-yellow in a split-complementary color scheme is wonderful with the cool blue-violet temperature change enhancing the design. This gorgeous color plan can be seen in sunrises and sunsets throughout the year. Golden-yellow is used in a split-complementary color plan in Delectable Mountains on page 47 and Dutch Mill on page 104.

Golden-Yellow and Its Unexpected Triadic Partners

Aqua blue and fuchsia are golden-yellow's natural triadic partners, and their hues are quite lovely together. A fabric selection is shown at the right. Delectable Mountains shows golden-yellow with its triadic partners on page 47.

Delectable Mountains
Split-Complementary

Split-Complementary

Delectable Mountains
Triadic

Triadic

Triadic

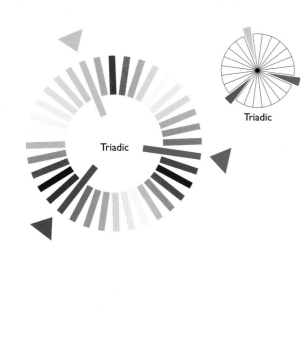

Triadic
Golden-Yellow, Aqua
Blue, and Fuchsia

CHIC CHARTREUSE—YELLOW WITH A TINGE OF GREEN

Chartreuse is a yellow hue with a tinge of green. Nature uses chartreuse to color flowers, leaves, seedpods, seaweed, and tropical birds. Some colorings are pure, while others are softly subtle. This color seems utterly unexpected when we see it in nature. Chartreuse is often used as a highlight in sunlit designs.

Chartreuse's tints are softer than those from the yellow family. They appear quite luminous. Dark chartreuse shades remind me of the deep, dark moss, ferns, and darkened brush found in forests. They are beautiful components of designs which showcase a natural setting. Chartreuse tones are very becoming as accents for quiet nature scenes. They can be wintry and calming. Photos 33B, 35B, and 68B show quilts using chartreuse in a strong role.

Monochromatic Chartreuse

Pure chartreuse can be seen with its other family members in the tint, shade, and tone scales shown at the right.

Duck & Ducklings
Monochromatic

The hues on this page can be used monochromatically or they may be used in any other color scheme that includes chartreuse.

Tints (chartreuse + white)

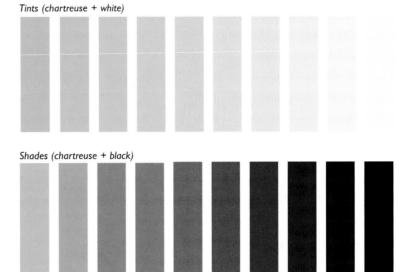

Shades (chartreuse + black)

Tones (pure chartreuse + gray)

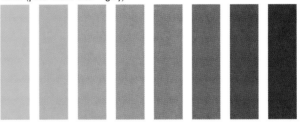

Tones (light chartreuse + gray)

Tones (dark chartreuse + gray)

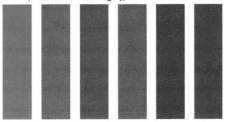

Chartreuse in Its Most Beautiful State —With Its Complementary Partner

Chartreuse is used often as a natural accent. Chartreuse and red-violet are a very striking twosome. Chartreuse really zings in designs with its complement.

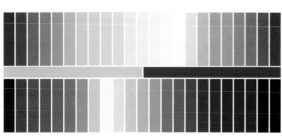

Complementary

Duck and Ducklings
Complementary

Complementary

Chartreuse and Its Analogous Partners

When chartreuse is used analogously, it often is combined with yellow and yellow-green to create a soft, subtle effect. It can also be expanded to a wider color range (see quilt photo 68B). The dogwood blossom and the magnolia pod are examples of such coloring. Chartreuse is used in an analogous role in Spinning Around the Block on page 46, Delectable Mountains on page 47, and Star Stretch on page 63.

Duck and Ducklings
Analogous

Analogous

Analogous

Analogous
Chartreuse

Chartreuse and Its Split-Complementary Options

Chartreuse's split-complementary color combination with red-violet provides a wonderful contrast in temperature change. A split-complementary fabrics selection is shown at the right. Chartreuse is used in split-complementary color schemes in Spinning Around the Block on page 46, Delectable Mountains on page 47, and Star Stretch on page 63.

Split-Complementary

Duck and Ducklings
Split-Complementary

Chartreuse and Its Triadic Partners

Cerulean blue (sky blue) and blue-red lie equal distances from chartreuse. A fabric selection of this dynamic triad is shown on page 114. Chartreuse is paired with its triadic partners in Storm at Sea (nine-patch) on page 119.

Triadic

Triadic

Duck and Ducklings
Triadic

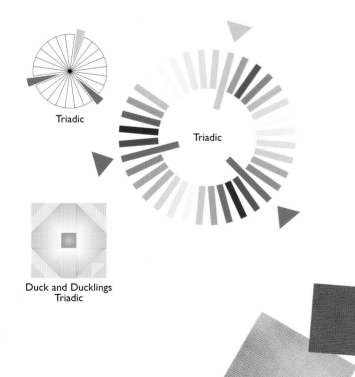

Split-Complementary
Chartreuse with Red-Violet

SPINNING AROUND THE BLOCK

(nine-patch pattern) in four different yellow color schemes

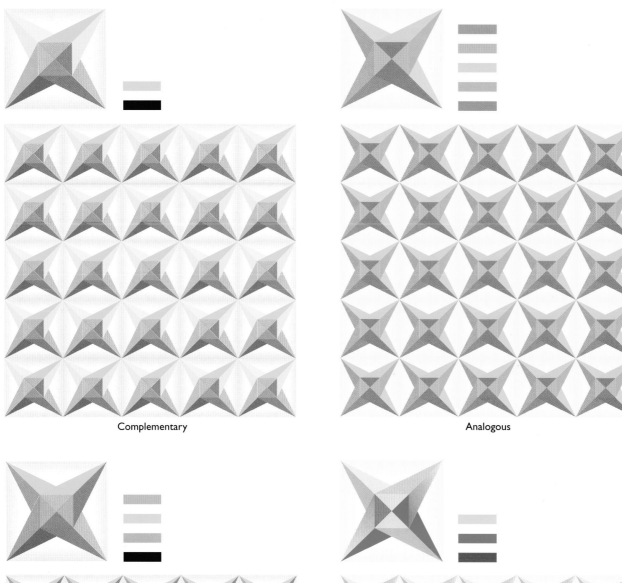

Complementary

Analogous

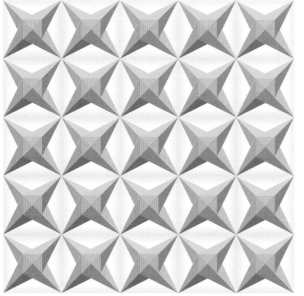

Split-Complementary

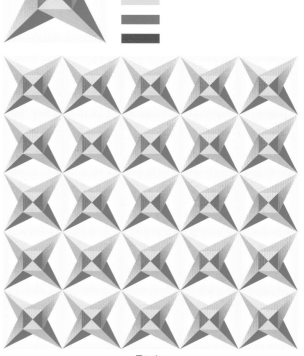

Triadic

DELECTABLE MOUNTAINS

(four-patch pattern) in four different golden-yellow color schemes

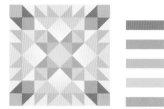

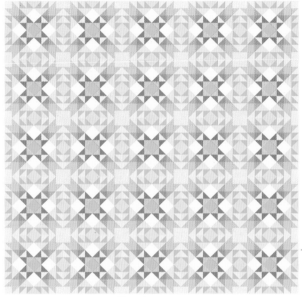

Complementary

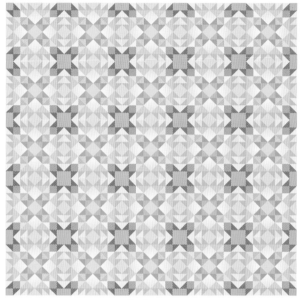

Analogous

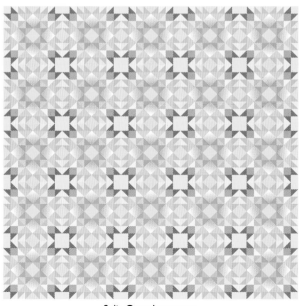

Split-Complementary

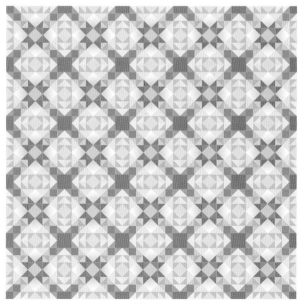

Triadic

chapter four

GORGEOUS GREENS

green
yellow-green
spring green
blue-green
aqua green

Green is the dominant color in most landscapes. Lush gardens, gently rolling farmlands, tree-lined country roads, lakes the color of emeralds, dense forest lands, silky moss, swiftly moving mountain streams, freshly-mowed lawns, wooded hideaways, new spring leaves, and deep seawater all give us glimpses of the various hues of green.

This chapter is divided into five color sections: green, yellow-green, spring green, blue-green, and aqua green. Pure green is a beautiful color, but it is not as prevalent in nature as other greens. Conversely, nature uses numerous warm yellow-green hues. They range from new leaves gently unfolding on their branches to the boughs of the vast Douglas Fir trees. Our forests, parklands, and gardens also display spring greens throughout. Blue-green vegetation makes a wonderful contrast to the other greens. Aqua greens are rare in our vegetation; they more often grace nature in sparkling water. There are many gorgeous green gemstones in our earth, including jade, emeralds, and aquamarine. The earth is truly filled with glorious greens!

Choose your favorite green, then head for that chapter section. Once you have decided which color scheme you wish to use, review its guidelines in Chapter Two. If you want to review ideas about using values, selecting the colors for a specific mood or season, playing with temperature, or any other basic color hints, refer to Chapter One.

GLORIOUS GREEN AND ITS CHOICES

Pure green is the middle color between yellow and turquoise on the color wheel. The soft green tints exude a fragile, delicate feeling. The dark green shades are rich and beautiful. These are the colors of shaded leaves and luscious wilderness. The toned-green hues of winter imagery are very gentle.

Monochromatic Green

A monochromatic color scheme can be made up of green with any of its tints, tones, and shades.

**Stepping Stones
Monochromatic**

The hues on this page can be used monochromatically or they may be used in any other color scheme that includes green.

Tints (green + white)

Shades (green + black)

Tones (pure green + gray)

Tones (light green + gray)

Tones (dark green + gray)

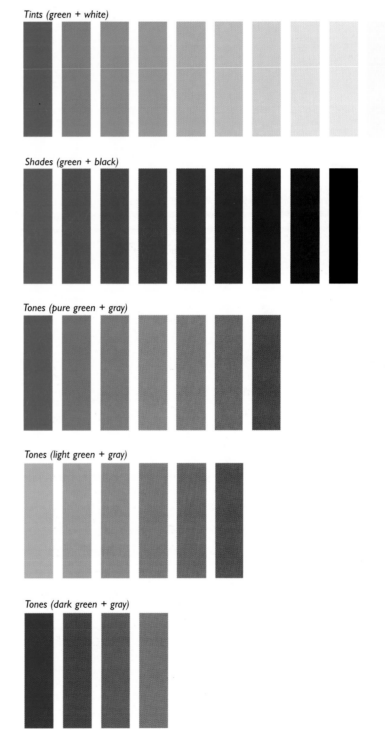

Green and Its Complement Magenta

Green's complementary color is magenta. These colors are beautiful together.

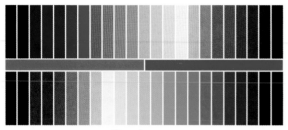

Complementary

An interesting note: Although many of us learned that red is green's complement, you can see that red does not lie directly across from green on the color wheel. Instead, magenta is opposite green. If you use magenta with green, you will have a more beautiful design than if you use red with green.

A quilt setting of Stepping Stones in a complementary color plan is shown on page 62. A fabric selection is shown at right.

Stepping Stones
Complementary

Complementary

Not Complementary

Complementary
Magenta and Green

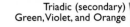

Green and Its Analogous Colors

The analogous color possibilities for green are numerous—and wonderful. Three, five, or seven hues can be selected. Stepping Stones on page 62 and Star Stretch on page 63 display analogous colorings with green.

Analogous

Stepping Stones
Analogous

Analogous

Using Green in Split-Complementary Color Schemes

Green is beautiful in a split-complementary color scheme with analogous hues and complementary magenta. Page 117 shows a split-complementary fabric selection with green as the complement. Split-complementary settings of Stepping Stones and Star Stretch are shown on pages 62 and 63.

Split-Complementary

Stepping Stones
Split-Complementary

Green's Triadic Partnership

Green's triadic partners are orange and violet. They, as well as the hues from their families, work beautifully together. A triadic fabric selection is shown below. Stepping Stones is set in a green triadic color plan on page 62.

Triadic

Triadic

Stepping Stones
Triadic

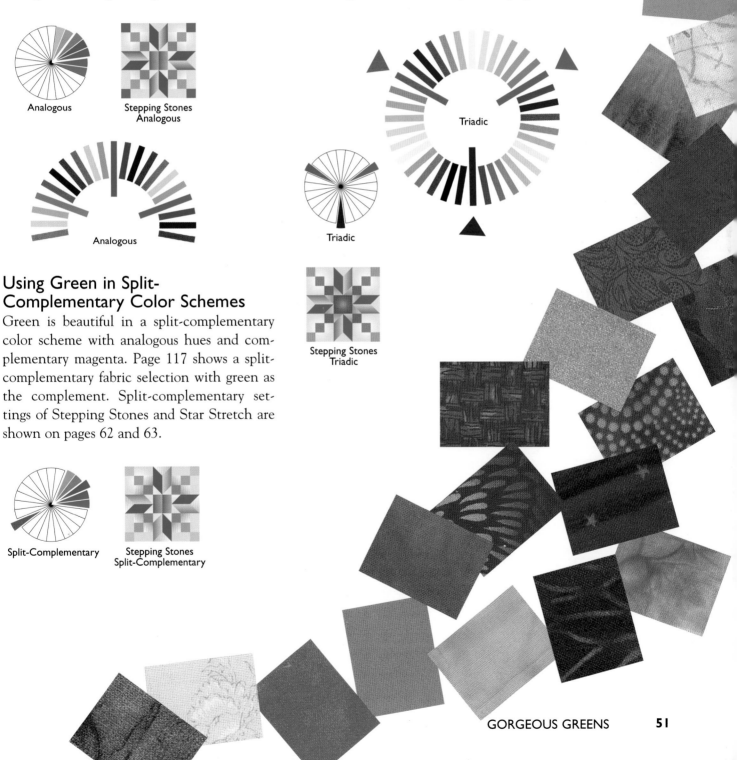

THE BRILLIANT YELLOW-GREEN FAMILY

Brilliant yellow-green is the warmest green on the color wheel. Our forests, parks, and gardens are filled with scores of yellow-green-leafed plants and trees. Yellow-green lies halfway between yellow and green, so it vibrates with yellow's energy. In nature, this dominant green color creates a sun-drenched effect. The tint scale shows yellow-green's lightest hues. The darkest greens can be seen in its shade scale. Many evergreen trees display these greens. When yellow-green has been toned (grayed), the colors become muted and more subdued. Often low-valued toned hues are seen in forests. The soft, lightly grayed green hues reflect the colors of stones found in the mountains or near the water.

Yellow-Green in a Monochromatic Color Scheme

If you wish to work in yellow-green's mono-chromatic color scheme, use only hues from this family.

Formal Garden
Monochromatic

The hues on this page can be used monochromatically or they may be used in any other color scheme that includes yellow-green.

Tints (yellow-green + white)

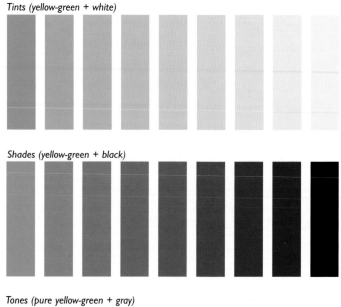

Shades (yellow-green + black)

Tones (pure yellow-green + gray)

Tones (light yellow-green + gray)

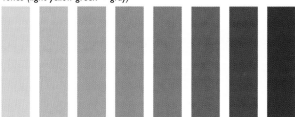

Tones (dark yellow-green + gray)

Yellow-Green and Its Complement

Purple lies opposite yellow-green on the color wheel. Purple can really zing when combined with yellow-green hues. Page 99 shows a complementary fabric selection. Nancy's Fancy on page 105 shows yellow-green in a complementary relationship.

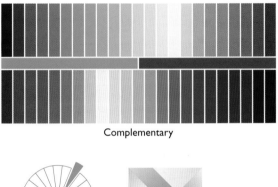

Complementary

Complementary

Formal Garden
Complementary

Analogous Yellow-Green

Yellow-green can be used in several analogous combinations. With yellow-green in the center position, you can vary the number of analogous colors from three, five, or seven families. Stepping Stones on page 62 and Star Stretch on page 63 use yellow-green analogously.

Analogous

Formal Garden
Analogous

Analogous

Using Yellow-Green in a Split-Complementary Color Scheme

Chartreuse, yellow-green, and spring green blend with purple to create a fantastic temperature shift in a split-complementary color plan. These colors vibrate with excitement. You can shift the complements so yellow-green plays the role of the complementary color, as purple works closely with fuchsia and red-violet. Yellow-green is shown in a split-complementary color scheme in the pattern Nancy's Fancy on page 105.

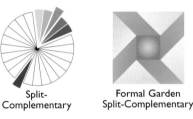

Split-
Complementary

Formal Garden
Split-Complementary

Yellow-Green and Its Triadic Partners

Blue and red are the spirited triadic partners of yellow-green. These colors create dynamic statements when combined with their tints, tones, and shades. A fabric selection is shown on page 80. Yellow-green is shown in a triadic color plan with the pattern Laurel Wreath on page 90.

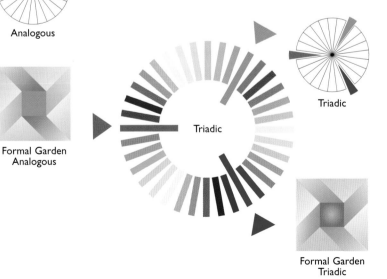

Triadic

Triadic

Formal Garden
Triadic

REFRESHING SPRING GREEN

Spring green has a mild hint of yellow in its makeup. This is to be expected, since it is a color that lies relatively close to yellow. Sometimes this color is called grass green. The tints are gorgeous. Mint green is readily recognized. Chocolate chip mint ice cream's coloring is a tinted hue of spring green. Our forests are filled with trees that show spring green's shaded hues. The subtle tones are fairly muted.

Spring Green and Its Monochromatic Possibilities

A spring green monochromatic design will have a refreshing quality.

Star Stretch
monochromatic

The hues on this page can be used monochromatically or they may be used in any other color scheme that includes spring-green.

Tints (spring green + white)

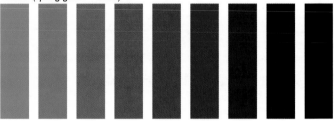

Shades (spring green + black)

Tones (pure spring green + gray)

Tones (light spring green + gray)

Tones (dark spring green + gray)

Spring Green and Its Complement Fuchsia

The complement of spring green is fuchsia, a color that lies between magenta and purple. The luscious comingling of this pair's hues make this a very attractive complement to use in a design. You can see spring green with fuchsia in Star Stretch on page 63.

Star Stretch
Complementary

Complementary

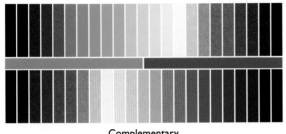

Complementary

Spring Green and Its Analogous Possibilities

You have several analogous possibilities using spring green as the dominant feature in a three-, five-, or seven-color design. An analogous fabric selection is shown at the right. Stepping Stones on page 62 and Star Stretch on page 63 use spring green analogously.

Analogous

Analogous

Star Stretch
Analogous

Analogous
Spring Green

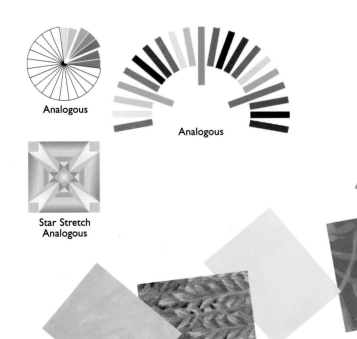

Spring Green and Its Beautiful Split-Complementary Combinations

The analogous combination of spring green with its temperature-shifting complement fuchsia can be stunning.

Split-
Complementary

Star Stretch
Split-Complementary

You can see a split-complementary color plan with Stepping Stones and Star Stretch on pages 62 and 63. A fabric selection using this great color combination is shown at the right.

Split-Complementary
Spring Green with Fuchsia

The Triadic Partners

Spring green's triadic partners are blue-violet and orange-red. What a dynamic partnership this is! Spring green is used as a triadic partner in Star Stretch on page 63 and Dutch Mill on page 104.

Triadic

Triadic

Star Stretch
Triadic

COOL BLUE-GREEN AND ITS NATURAL COLOR PARTNERS

Blue-green is a luscious, cool hue. Many shade-loving plants have blue-green leaves. Sea-foam, a tint of blue-green, is very soothing. The quilts shown in photos 35A and 67A use blue-green as a major color.

Blue-green and Its Monochromatic Hues

Pure blue-green and its tints, shades, and tones can be used in a monochromatic setting to great advantage because of their freshness. You can use the pure hue and any of the tints, shades, and tones.

Woven Star
monochromatic

The hues on this page can be used monochromatically or they may be used in any other color scheme that includes blue-green.

Tints (blue-green + white)

Shades (blue-green + black)

Tones (pure blue-green + gray)

Tones (light blue-green + gray)

Tones (dark blue-green + gray)

Blue-Green and Its Complement Blue-Red

Blue-green's complementary partner is blue-red. These two colors are absolutely glorious with each other, as you can see with the hue selection below.

Woven Star
Complementary

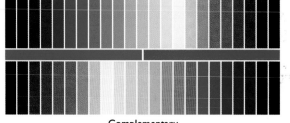

Complementary

Complementary

Analogous
Blue-Green

Blue-Green and Its Analogous Options

You can create wonderful designs with blue-green and its analogous neighbors using three, five, or seven hues. An analogous fabric selection is shown at the right. The Stepping Stones design on page 62 and Star Stretch on page 63 show blue-green used analogously.

Woven Star
Analogous

Analogous

Analogous

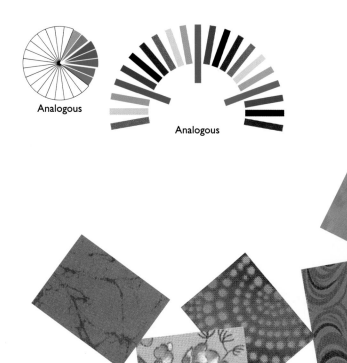

Blue-Green and Its Split-Complementary Possibilities

The split-complementary color scheme of spring green, green, blue-green, aqua green, and aqua blue is lovely. Blue-red is its natural temperature shift. A fabric selection is shown at the right. You can see split-complementary settings using blue-green in Stepping Stones on page 62 and Star Stretch on page 63.

Blue-Green's Triadic Partners

Blue-green's triadic partners are red-violet and yellow-orange. This is another dynamic partnership. You can see blue-green and its triadic partners in Through the Looking Glass on page 129.

Woven Star
Split-Complementary

Split-Complementary

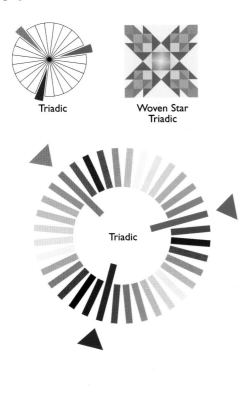

Split-Complementary
Blue-Green with Blue-Red

Triadic

Woven Star
Triadic

Triadic

SPARKLING AQUA GREEN AND ITS LOVELY COMPANIONS

Aqua green is a breathtakingly beautiful color. It seems almost unreal in nature, but it isn't. Speckled here and there throughout the world are amazing aqua green lakes hidden among vast areas of untouched wilderness. Far away from these awesome natural settings, you can cast your eyes on aqua green hues in the warm tropical waters of the Atlantic Ocean.

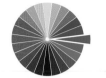

Aqua Green and Its Monochromatic Hues

Pure aqua green and any of its tints, shades, and tones can be used in a monochromatic design.

Stone Mason's Puzzle
Monochromatic

The hues on this page can be used monochromatically or they may be used in any other color scheme that includes aqua green.

Tints (aqua green + white)

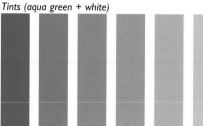

Shades (aqua green + black)

Tones (pure aqua green + gray)

Tones (light aqua green + gray)

Tones (dark aqua green + gray)

Aqua Green and Its Complement Red

Aqua green and its complementary partner red are fantastic together. They are much prettier together than the commonly used (although not complementary) red and green.

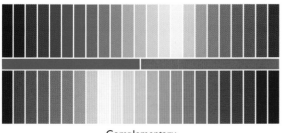

Complementary

Complementary

Stone Mason's Puzzle
Complementary

Aqua Green and Its Analogous Options

You can create wonderful analogous designs with aqua green using three, five, or seven colors. Aqua green can be positioned on either end of the analogous range. Aqua green is shown analogously in Stepping Stones on page 62.

Analogous

Stone Mason's Puzzle
Analogous

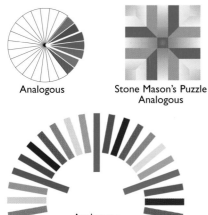

Analogous

Aqua Green and Its Split-Complementary Possibilities

Aqua green is stunning in its split-complementary color plan, which uses blue-green, aqua green, aqua blue, and red. You can see aqua green in a split-complementary scheme on page 62 in Stepping Stones.

Split-
Complementary

Stone Mason's Puzzle
Split-Complementary

Aqua Green's Triadic Partners

Aqua green's triadic partners are purple and orange-yellow. What a beautiful design they can create! A fabric selection can be seen on page 100. On pages 105 and 128 aqua green can be seen in other triadic color designs.

Triadic

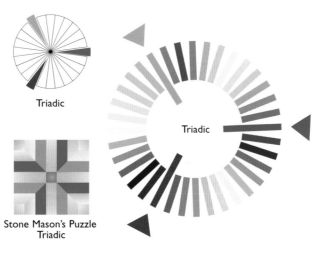

Stone Mason's Puzzle
Triadic

Triadic

STEPPING STONES

(4-patch pattern) in four different green color schemes

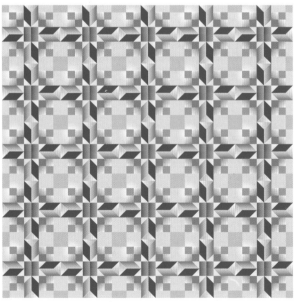

Complementary

Analogous

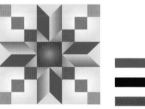

Split-Complementary

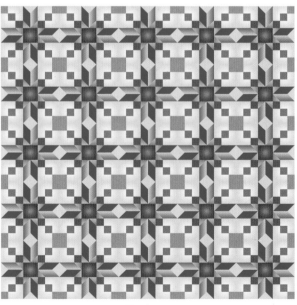

Triadic

STAR STRETCH (7-patch pattern) in four different spring green color schemes

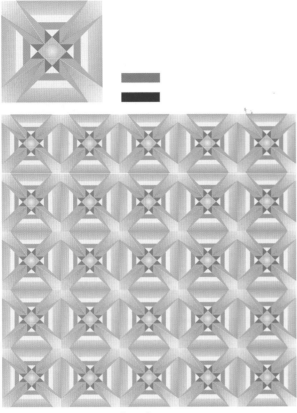

Complementary

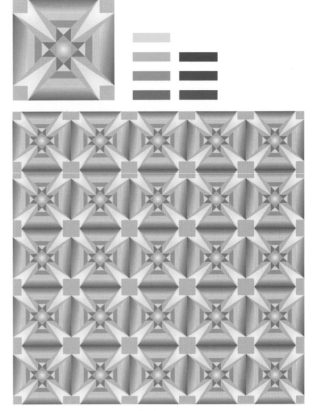

Analogous

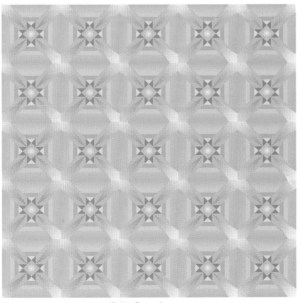

Split-Complementary

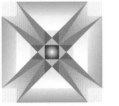

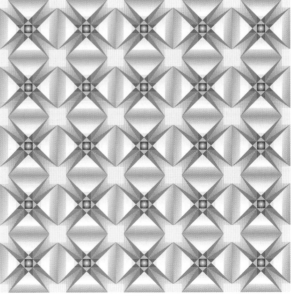

Triadic

AN EXHIBIT
OF COLORFUL QUILTS

64A STARRY WAY, 1996, 53" × 41"
Noelle Evans, Hillsboro, Oregon

This Road to Paradise design was inspired by
Beatrice F. Johnson's quilt *When You Wish Upon a
Star*, as seen in Lynn Kough's *Stretching Tradition*.
(Photo: Ken Wagner)

64C MARINERS AT SEA, 1998, 82" × 106"
Ann Jenson, Richland, Washington

This blue quilt uses strong value
changes to create a striking design.
(Photo: Mark Roberts)

64B   THE BLUES OF CARMEL, 1995, 50" × 59"
Elizabeth Eastmond, Riverside, California

This Thousand Pyramids quilt uses an
analogous color scheme to create its design.
(Photo: Ken Wagner)

65A WINTER, 1998, 40" × 36"
Lesly-Claire Greenberg, Fairfax, Virginia

Winter, made from a one-patch pattern, is created in the soft, subtle toned hues. The quilt was made into a Torah mantle. It now resides in the Ark on a sacred scroll. Owner: Temple B'nai Shalom, Fairfax Station, Virginia. Machine quilter: Joanne Fiorino.
(Photo: Jason Horowitz/Mirror Ball Studio)

65B COLORWASH DIAMOND WEDDING RING, 1998, 90" × 90"
Sylvia I. King, Pasco, Washington

To create this subtle color blend, Sylvia hand dyed all the fabric. This quilt was inspired by Shar Jorgenson's TV program about Wedding Ring quilts.
(Photo: Ken Wagner)

65C INDIAN ORANGE PEEL VARIATION, 1997, 61" × 61"
Barbara Schneider, McHenry, Illinois

The strong value contrasts in *Indian Orange Peel Variation* sharpen the design, while the spontaneous color changes cause the design to vibrate. The quilt is made from Karen Stone's Indian Orange Peel pattern.
(Photo: John Moorer)

66A FEATHERLIGHT, 1998, 77" x 93"
Mariya A. Waters, Ivanhoe, Australia

Featherlight is the second in a series
of Mariya's distorted pinwheel designs.
The overlapping of the circular pinwheels
creates the illusion of depth.
(Photo: Robert Claxton)

66C PRIMARY STARS II, 1998, 46" x 62"
Diana Voyer, Victoria, British Columbia, Canada

This simple historic Variable Star pattern
with its striking color and value changes
throughout the quilt's surface appears quite
contemporary. The concentric quilting
further enhances the quilt's drama.
(Photo: Ken Wagner)

66B HEATHER'S BLUE GLASS COLLECTION,
88" x 104"
Sandy Corry, Inverell, Australia

This lovely blended design combines the blocks Hidden
Star and Milky Way from Jinny Beyer's *Patchwork Portfolio*.
(Photo: Anthony Elliott)

67A WHAT'S THE STORY,
MORNING GLORY, 1997, 53" × 53"
Charlotte Warr Andersen, Salt Lake City, Utah

Depth is created in two ways: by overlapping objects
and by using light, toned fabrics in the background.
(Photo: T. Anastasion)

67B OFF SQUARE, 1998, 37" × 37"
Lynn Underwood, Saskatoon, Saskatchewan, Canada

This variation of a Log Cabin quilt is an adaptation from
a cushion in Kaffe Fassett's *Glorious Patchwork* book. The
tint scale appears to play a dominant role in this design.
(Photo: Grant Kernan, A.K. Photos)

67C ALLERGIC TO BROOMS, 1993, 40" × 45"
Charlotte McFarland, Victoria, British Columbia, Canada

A whimsical quilt shows how overlapping objects creates
depth. (Photo: Ken Wagner)

67D DRAGON DANCE, 1998, 72¾" × 81½"
Lynn Underwood, Saskatoon, Saskatchewan, Canada

Inspired by Karen Stone's *New York Beauty* book, Lynn created a colorful path that moves throughout the quilt's body.
(Photo: Grant Kernan)

68A MESSENGER #2, 1996, 52" x 67"
Caryl Bryer Fallert, Oswego, Illinois

In *Messenger #2*, the blending of curved lines
and transparency creates a dynamic design. The
play of warm and cool colors is very effective.
(Photo: Courtesy of the artist)

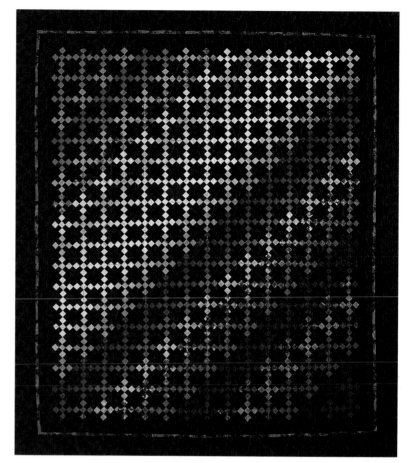

68B NINE-PATCH GONE UPTOWN,
1998, 78" x 92"
Kit Willey, Niagara-on-the-Lake, Ontario, Canada

This colorful quilt was made from a Nine-
Patch block and an alternate plain block.
Value change creates the lustrous illusion.
(Photo: Sharon Risedorph)

68C FLYING FREE #2, 1995, 82" x 93"
Caryl Bryer Fallert, Oswego, Illinois

Here organic imagery of vines, leaves,
flowers, and vegetables from Caryl's
garden are abstractly intertwined. Caryl
superbly creates depth and luster through
color scale and value changes.
(Photo: Courtesy of the artist)

69A JEWEL FIRE, 1996, 89" × 108"
Gwendolyn A. Magee, Jackson, Mississippi

This gorgeous quilt uses the historic
block Endless Chain. The intense,
pure colors surrounded by toned
hues create hints of luminosity.
(Photo: Errol Dillon)

69C SUMMER DAWN, 1997, 84" × 84"
Kaye Rhodes, Annandale, Virginia

This off-set Log Cabin quilt is stunning with its split-
complementary colors vibrating outwardly. Depth
and luminosity are created through color play.
(Photo: Ken Wagner)

69B GRETA'S QUILT, 1999, 75" × 75"
Dana Matthews, Moccasin, California

Dana uses the pattern as a vehicle to
create a scenic illusion for her daughter's
quilt. Depth, luminosity, and transparency
play throughout the quilt's design.
(Photo: Ken Wagner)

70A EDUCATION, 1998, 90" × 102"
Nellouise S. Sherman, Lawrence, Kansas

Nellouise Sherman and her son Barry designed this quilt with depth, highlights, and shadows. They combined and expanded the patterns Tumbling Star by Virginia Walton and Quilted Puzzle by Judy Mathieson. Machine quilted by Barbara Eikmeier.

(Photo: Jon Blumb)

70C RISE AND SHINE, INNER CITY, 1997, 76" × 96"
Martha W. Ginn, Hattiesburg, Mississippi

Martha used the pattern Inner City to create three-dimensionality, highlights, and shadows. This quilt's color play symbolizes neighborhoods touching and blending as the sun rises over the city.

(Photo: Brent Wallace)

70B LOG CABIN QUILT, 1996, 89" × 89"
Helen Remick, Seattle, Washington

Intense red fabrics, contrasting with neutral hues from the total value spectrum make this a stunning log cabin design.

(Photo: Ken Wagner)

71A CROSSING THE BORDERS, 1993, 81" x 81"
Irene MacWilliam, Belfast, Northern Ireland

This analogous Pineapple Log Cabin quilt is designed so the Flying Geese could flow over the block boundaries.
(Photo: Courtesy of the artist)

71B BURNING THE MIDNIGHT OIL, 1997, 56" x 62"
Beth Miller, Kambah, ACT, Australia

The contrasting warm/cool colors of *Burning the Midnight Oil*, a Courthouse steps Log Cabin design, is very striking. The floated border accentuates the drama.
(Photo: Andrew Sikorski).

71C CELESTIAL WONDER, 1998, 61" x 48"
Jackie Frovarp, Saskatoon,
Saskatchewan, Canada

Celestial Wonder is a spectacular log cabin quilt that appears lustrous with its value changes.
(Photo: Grant Kernan, A.K. Photos)

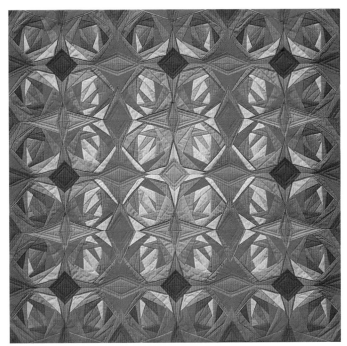

71D ROSE TRELLIS, 1998, 24" x 24"
Irene MacWilliam, Belfast, Northern Ireland

Irene created the illusions of depth and luminosity by surrounding clear colors with toned hues.
(Photo: Courtesy of the artist)

72A SEPTEMBER'S MY FAVORITE,
1996, 49" × 39"
Sandy Boyd, Glenwood Springs, Colorado

This autumnal quilt uses warm shades for
its dominant color scale. Overlapping objects
and using less distinct colors in the background
create the appearance of depth.
(Photo: Marc Schuman)

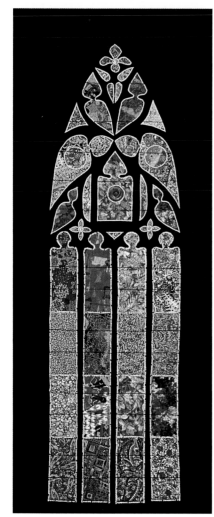

72B CHURCH WINDOW #2, 1997, 26" × 58"
Sandy Corry, Inverell, Australia

A stunning church window is created
primarily from rich, warm shades, so as
to elicit the glorious colors of autumn.
(Photo: Anthony Elliott)

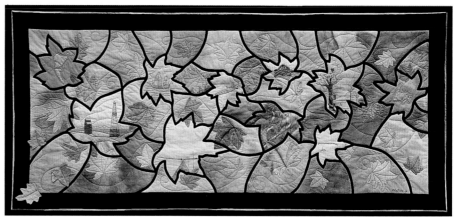

72C CANADA IS, 1993, 56" × 25"
Susan Duffield, Sidney, British Columbia, Canada

Transparency is evident in this split-complementary
color plan. Several Canadian vignettes are subtly placed
throughout the design. *(Photo: Ken Wagner)*

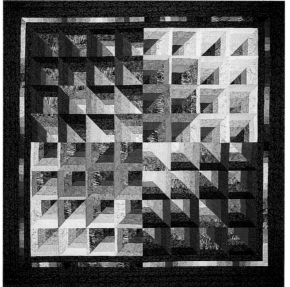

72D AZTEC SIZZLE, 1995, 57" × 57"
Clare Claridge, Mid Glamorgan, Wales

Clare has created a striking
design inspired by Margaret
Miller's *Strips That Sizzle*.
(Photo: Huw Evans)

73A ANOTHER FENCE, 1998, 62" × 42"
Sandy Boyd, Glenwood Springs, Colorado

Overlapping color temperature and great fabric selection create dimensionality in this summer imagery quilt.

(Photo: Mark Schuman)

73B BASKETS, 1999, 50" × 50"
Diana Voyer, Victoria, British Columbia, Canada

Baskets was inspired by a basket quilt in Alex Anderson's *Quilts for Fabric Lovers*. Moving background values from dark to light further enhances the design.

(Photo: Ken Wagner)

74A SEASONAL LIGHT, 1996, 72" × 85"
Mariya A. Waters, Ivanhoe, Australia

This fascinating quilt creates its movement and three-dimensionality from the pinwheel pattern's grid distortion. Value change enhances depth. The turquoise appears to float above the warm hues.
(Photo: Robert Claxton)

74B WEAVE NINE, 1999, 60" × 60"
Reynola Pakusich, Bellingham, Washington

This unbelievably dynamic Snail's Trail quilt is beautifully enhanced with illusions of depth, luster, and transparency.
(Photo: Louise Harris)

74C QUEST FOR FIRE, 1994, 30" × 26"
Caryl Bryer Fallert, Oswego, Illinois

The design is enhanced by the use of strong pure hues set against toned hues, which allows the viewer to focus on the dramatic features. Transparency is created through fabric and metallic thread work.
(Photo: Courtesy of the artist)

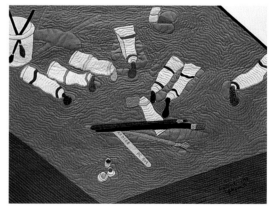

74D THE STUDIO, 1998, 29" × 22"
Beth P. Gilbert, Buffalo Grove, Illinois

This original design uses the tone scale in a dominant role. Overlapping elements enhance the quilt's three-dimensionality.
(Photo: Ken Wagner)

75A CUPS OF SCRAPS, 1997, 50" × 35"
Madelon Carels, Amsterdam,
The Netherlands

This tea cup quilt creates great interest
because of its use of fabric. It was inspired by
a quilt seen in *Patchwork Quilt Tsushin*, 1997.
(Photo: Gerard van Yperem)

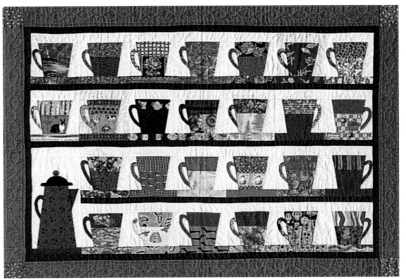

75B CREWEL WHIRL, 1996, 89" × 89"
Patrice Perkins Creswell, Austin, Texas

This awesome quilt is beautifully colored in
warm, rich shades, giving it an autumnal feeling.
Crewel Whirl's design is based on both a
mariner's compass and crewel embroidery.
(Photo: Beth T. Kennedy)

75C NEW YORK BEAUTY, 1998, 68" × 68"
Kay Lettau, Annandale, Virginia

This New York Beauty quilt is stunning with
its warm analogously colored shades.
(Photo: Ken Wagner)

75D LONE STAR, 1996, 67" × 67"
Barbara Schneider, McHenry, Illinois

Lone Star is in subtle blends of warm hues
with touches of dark blue for contrast. The
value changes are quite effective, helping to
create color movement and transparency.
(Photo: John W. Moore)

76A THE CHARM SCHOOL, 1998, 58" × 70"
Kaye Rhodes, Annandale, Virginia

This beautifully analogous quilt is made from
1440 half-square triangles. Each triangle is cut
from a different fabric. Kaye was inspired by
Sharyn Craig's "Design challenge: Triangulation"
in *Traditional Quiltworks Magazine #17*.
(Photo: Ken Wagner)

76B PASTEL PINWHEELS, 1995, 46" × 58"
Elaine Martin, North Platte, Nebraska

Elaine has used high-valued tones to
create this scrap quilt's design.
(Photo: George Hipple Photography)

76C NIGHT SKY, 1996, 47" × 47"
Nancy A. Nelson, Schenectady, New York

The pure turquoise and magenta Mariner's
Compasses are striking in their purity in *Night Sky*.
(Photo: Ken Wagner)

76D DANCING TWILIGHT, 1984, 30" × 36"
Joen Wolfrom, Fox Island, Washington

Transparency was created as this off-centered
Pinwheel pattern moved from light to dark.
(Photo: Ken Wagner)

chapter five
BLISSFUL BLUES

blue
cerulean blue
turquoise
aqua blue

The blue spectrum is a major player in our world's background. We most often see blue as the color everything else is set against. The blue spectrum is a striking contrast to the multitude of other colors in nature. Often blues create refreshing, airy, and serene moods. They can suggest sophistication, elegance, and formality. Overall, blues are colors of peace and hope. For your convenience, this chapter has been divided into four major blue sections: blue, cerulean blue, turquoise, and aqua blue.

Warm blues can be brilliant and dazzling. Dark blues, contrasting with warm colors, can be dramatic (see photo 71B). Light blues give an airy, fresh feeling. Grayed blues can be atmospheric and fragile. Light, grayed blues easily suggest a wintry scene or an icy mood.

Being surrounded by blue tends to decrease muscle activity, blood pressure, respiration, and heart rate. Blue, then, is an excellent color for bedrooms and other rooms meant for rest and respite. If you wish to create a tranquil quilt, start with a blue family.

For your next blue project, select your favorite color and then choose the color scheme you would like to use. To learn about each color scheme's characteristics and guidelines go to Chapter Two. If you would like to review guidelines for color scales, values, intensity, or color temperature, turn to Chapter One.

BLISSFUL BLUE

Pure blue, a color lying halfway between turquoise and violet, is one of the most popular hues on the color wheel. Because pure blue is rather dark, it has numerous tints in its family. Our midday sky is often a blue tint. Whenever blue has black added to it, it becomes a shade. Navy blue is extremely popular as either a shade or a dark tone.

Monochromatic Blue

Blue is probably the most popular color to use in a monochromatic design. It is sophisticated, restful, and immensely beautiful. Besides pure blue, tints, shades, and tones may be used in your design.

Laurel Wreath
Monochromatic

The hues on this page can be used monochromatically or they may be used in any other color scheme that includes blue.

Tints (blue + white)

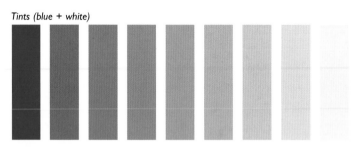

Shades (blue + black)

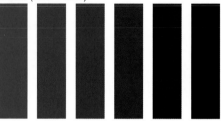

Tones (pure blue + gray)

Tones (light blue + gray)

Tones (dark blue + gray)

Analogous
Blue

Blue and Its Wonderful Complementary Partner

Blue is a lovely color, especially when it's partnered with orange-yellow, its complement. We often see this combination in early morning and evening skies. Although many of us learned differently, blue and orange are not complements, as they do not lie opposite each other on the color wheel. Blue is more beautifully partnered with orange-yellow. A fabric selection is shown on page 127. On page 90 the pattern Laurel Wreath shows blue in a complementary color plan.

Complementary

Not Complementary

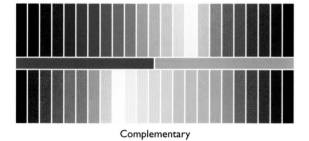

Complementary

Laurel Wreath
Complementary

Blue in Its Analogous Color Plan

Blue is very beautiful in an analogous color scheme. Blue can be the middle hue, or it can be positioned on either end of the analogous color range. You can see blue used analogously in Laurel Wreath on page 90. Photo 64C shows a quilt using blue analogously.

Laurel Wreath
Analogous

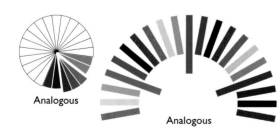

Analogous

Analogous

Blue and Its Split-Complementary Pals

The split-complementary color scheme for blue works very effectively. It not only looks wonderful with its analogous neighbors, but it is also greatly enhanced by the complementary temperature change of orange-yellow. Blue is used in a split-complementary color plan in Laurel Wreath on page 90.

Split-
Complementary

Laurel Wreath
Split-Complementary

Blue's Triadic Partners

Blue's triadic partners are red and yellow-green. Laurel Wreath is shown in a triadic setting on page 90. A fabric selection is shown at the right.

Triadic

Triadic

Laurel Wreath
Triadic

Many designs are created in blues and reds. This often results in a sense of something missing or of a visual imbalance. Since red and blue are not complements, they are not best paired together as two hues. Thus, if you want to use blue and red together, use them in a triadic rather than a dual partnership. The natural third partner is yellow-green. You will be surprised and delighted by the uplifting results. If you are apprehensive about adding yellow-green to your blue and red design, use it as an accent. You can use its soft tints, subtle tones, or rich shades with a touch of the pure hue.

Triadic
Blue, Red, and
Yellow-Green

BREATHTAKING CERULEAN BLUE—SKY BLUE

 If we stop to look above us during midday, we may be awed by the sky's glorious blue color. This beautiful blue, with its refreshing hint of warmth, is informally called sky blue. Formally, its name is cerulean blue. Cerulean blue lies between blue and turquoise on the color wheel. Both sky and water are often colored in cerulean blue. Many cultures use this lovely, warm blue in their designs. Scandinavian homes are often decorated with this blue.

Cerulean blue's popular tints can often be seen in home decor. Rich, dark shades are created when black is added to cerulean blue. When cerulean hues are toned, their intensity is lessened, whether they are light-, dark-, or medium-valued hues.

Monochromatic Cerulean Blue

Cerulean blue, the blue of endless skies, is beautiful in a monochromatic color scheme. Use the pure color and any of its tints, shades, and tones together. A small selection of cerulean blue fabric is shown below.

Cerulean Blue Fabrics

Dancing Star
Monochromatic

The hues on this page can be used monochromatically or they may be used in any other color scheme that includes cerulean blue.

Tints (cerulean blue + white)

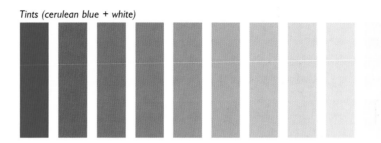

Shades (cerulean blue + black)

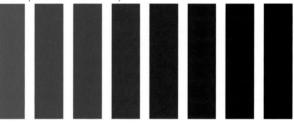

Tones (pure cerulean blue + gray)

Tones (light cerulean blue + gray)

Tones (dark cerulean blue + gray)

Cerulean Blue and Its Complement

Warm cerulean blue goes beautifully with yellow-orange, its complement. The color of juicy apricots and cantaloupe complements this blue immensely. Scores of sunrises and sunsets display this color combination. Cerulean blue is a complement in Through the Looking Glass on page 129.

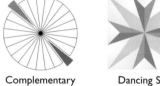

Complementary

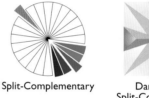

Complementary   Dancing Star
                    Complementary

Cerulean Blue's Analogous Possibilities

Cerulean blue is especially pretty when used with five analogous colors. Storm at Sea on page 89 and Dutch Mill on page 104 show cerulean blue in an analogous plan. Photo 64C shows an analogously colored quilt.

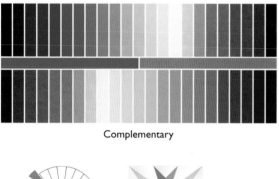

Analogous   Dancing Star Analogous

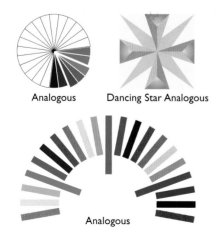

Analogous

Cerulean Blue and Its Split-Complementary Options

Cerulean blue looks great when combined with its neighboring colors along with its complement yellow-orange. The most usual combination places cerulean blue in the center analogous position with three or five colors. Cerulean blue can also be the complement to yellow-orange and its analogous neighbors. (See quilt photo 69B.) A fabric selection is shown on page 125. Dutch Mill on page 104 and Through the Looking Glass on page 129 use cerulean blue in split-complementary color plans.

Split-Complementary   Dancing Star
                          Split-Complementary

The Surprising Triadic Partners

Cerulean blue's triadic partners are blue-red and chartreuse. Another triadic setting can be seen in Storm at Sea on page 119. Page 114 shows a cerulean blue triadic fabric selection.

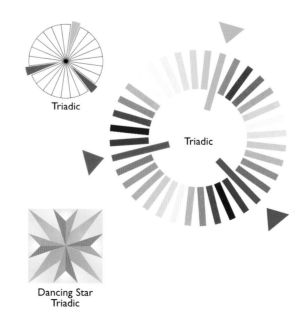

Triadic

Triadic

Dancing Star
Triadic

TRANQUIL TURQUOISE

Turquoise, one of the primary colors of the Ives color wheel, is a beautiful, much-loved color. Printers and photographers call this color cyan. Regardless of the name one uses, it is lovely. Its beauty flows throughout its family. The tint, shade, and tone scales are beautiful too. We see the tints in different parts of our earth. Turquoise and blue topaz are extraordinarily beautiful hues from the tint scale. Skies and waterways can be in turquoise hues. Dark turquoise shades and tones are rich and luscious. Interestingly, turquoise is a color almost everyone can wear, in one scale or another. Selected quilts using turquoise are shown in quilt photos 33C, 34A, 65B, and 141B.

Turquoise in a Monochromatic Statement

Use pure turquoise and its tints, shades and tones for a rich, striking design. Be sure to incorporate good value change when working with your monochromatic design.

Storm at Sea
Monochromatic

The hues on this page can be used monochromatically or they may be used in any other color scheme that includes turquoise.

Tints (turquoise + white)

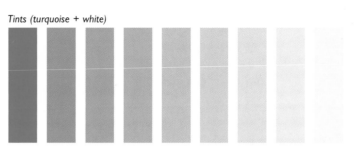

Shades (turquoise + black)

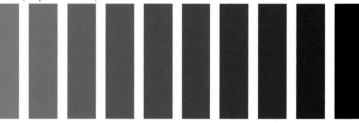

Tones (pure turquoise + gray)

Tones (light turquoise + gray)

Tones (dark turquoise + gray)

Turquoise and Its Glorious Complement Orange

Turquoise and orange are an amazing combination because this partnership creates a fire-and-ice effect with the heat of orange and the coolness of turquoise. Orange's soft orange-apricots, rusts, and browns are quite striking combined with turquoise hues. The sky is fantastic when it's filled with these two complements. A selection of fabrics is shown at the right. A complementary coloring of Storm at Sea is on page 89.

Storm at Sea
Complementary

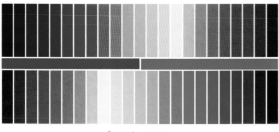

Complementary

Complementary

Complementary
Turquoise and Orange

Turquoise and Its Analogous Relatives

Turquoise looks smashing in its analogous settings. It can be positioned in the center or on either end of the color range. Use three, five, or seven color families. Storm at Sea on page 89 uses turquoise in an analogous setting.

Turquoise and Its Triadic Partnership

Along with magenta and yellow, turquoise is a member of the primary triadic color scheme. Turquoise is shown in triadic plans in Storm at Sea on page 89 and Spinning Around the Block on page 46.

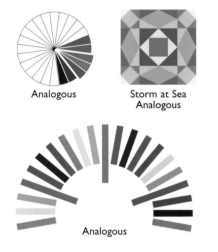

Analogous

Storm at Sea
Analogous

Analogous

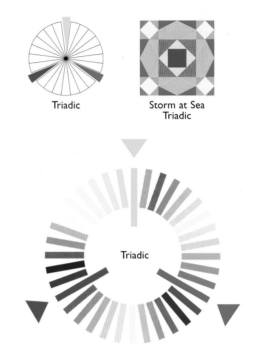

Triadic

Storm at Sea
Triadic

Triadic

Turquoise and Its Split-Complementary Options

In a split-complementary color plan, turquoise is generally placed in the center analogous position, while orange, its complement, is the temperature-shifting hue. Storm at Sea is shown in a split-complementary plan on page 89.

Split-
Complementary

Storm at Sea
Split-Complementary

SPARKLING AQUA BLUE

Aqua blue is a happy, bubbly color. Because it is rare in nature, aqua blue catches our immediate attention when we see it. Throughout the world, deep, cold, mountain lakes are colored aqua blue hues. Delicate robins' eggs are beautifully colored a tinted aqua blue. Shown at the right are some of aqua blue's delicate tints, rich shades, and subtle tones.

Aqua Blue's Monochromatic Color Plan

Combine pure aqua blue with its light, fragile tints and lovely dark shades for refreshing monochromatic designs. If you are interested in having a subtle presentation, however, use mostly tones in your fabric selection.

Yankee Puzzle
Monochromatic

The hues on this page can be used monochromatically or they may be used in any other color scheme that includes aqua blue.

Tints (aqua blue + white)

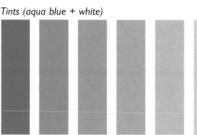

Shades (aqua blue + black)

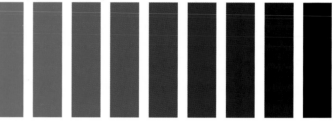

Tones (pure aqua blue + gray)

Tones (light aqua blue + gray)

Tones (dark aqua blue + gray)

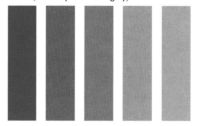

Aqua Blue and Its Complementary Color Scheme

Complementary color schemes are particularly beautiful when they combine two colors that symbolically remind us of warmth and coolness, as aqua blue and orange-red do. The combination of hues in their tinted and shaded form can be spectacular. Orange-red's tints are beautiful, soft orange corals. The rusts and browns are scrumptious. These hues are exciting with the aqua blue hues. Aqua blue is used as a complement in Bachelor Puzzle on page 118.

Yankee Puzzle
Complementary

Complementary

Analogous
Aqua Blue

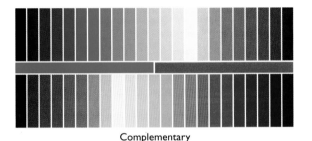

Complementary

Aqua Blue with Its Analogous Neighbors

If you love aqua blue, use this harmonic color plan with either three, five, or seven hues. Aqua blue is generally the middle hue, but it can be placed at either edge of the color range. An analogous fabric selection is shown at the right. Storm at Sea on page 89 shows aqua blue analogously.

Yankee Puzzle
Analogous

Analogous

Analogous

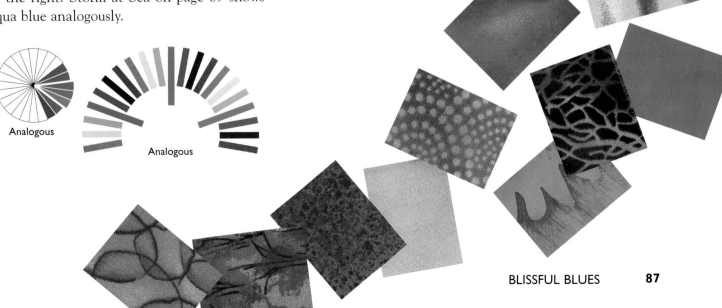

Aqua Blue with Its Split-Complementary Options

Aqua blue, aqua green, and turquoise are very beautiful together with orange-red. However, you may wish to expand the color range to five colors for more interest. Aqua blue and its analogous hues give a cool, watery effect with orange-red creating a touch of warmth. If you want a warmer design, use aqua blue as the complement to orange-red and its warm analogous neighbors. Aqua blue is used in a split-complementary color plan in Storm at Sea on page 89 and Bachelor's Puzzle on page 118.

Aqua Blue's Triadic Partners

Aqua blue, fuchsia, and golden-yellow are three colors that go together beautifully. They are natural partners because they lie equal distances away from each other. Delectable Mountains on page 47 uses aqua blue and its triadic partners.

Yankee Puzzle
Split-Complementary

Split-Complementary

Yankee Puzzle
Triadic

Triadic

Triadic

Split-Complementary
Aqua Blue with Orange-Red

STORM AT SEA (4-patch pattern) in four different turquoise color schemes

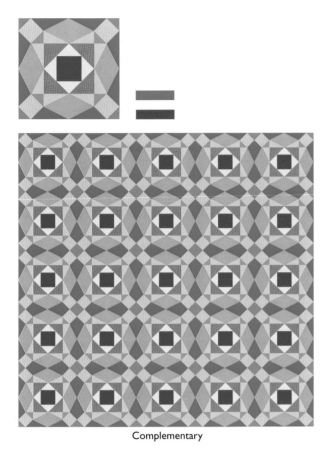

Complementary

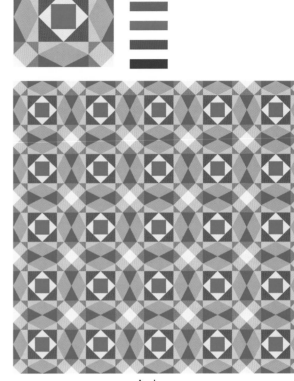

Analogous

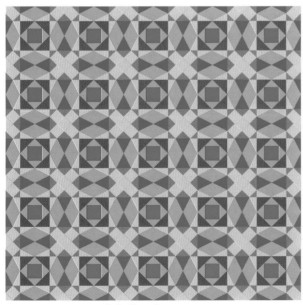

Split-Complementary

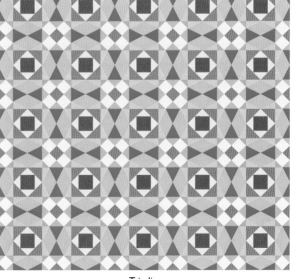

Triadic

LAUREL WREATH (4-patch pattern) in four different blue color schemes

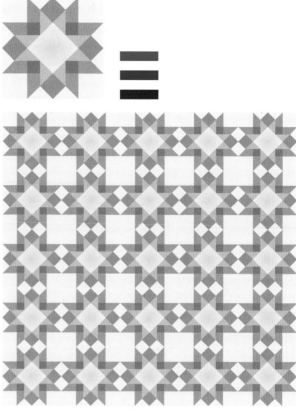

Complementary

Analogous

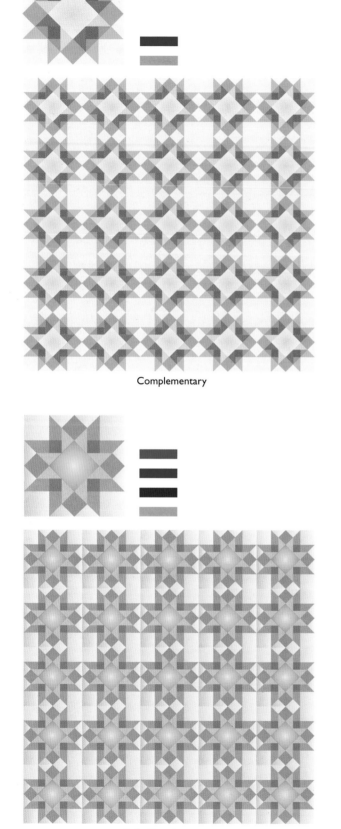

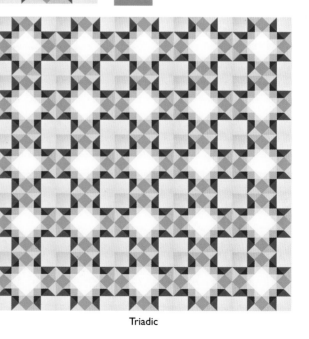

Split-Complementary

Triadic

chapter six

VERY ROYAL VIOLETS

violet
blue-violet
red-violet
purple
fuchsia

The violet-spectrum colors at the bottom of the color wheel are rich and magnificent. Centuries ago, these colors were the most difficult colors to obtain. Only the most elite could afford to wear garments or decorate their homes with these colors. They became the favorites of ancient rulers because of their rarity. These violet hues continue to be the colors of nobility. They are worn as symbols of high office or rank, imperial power, or high birth. These colors are stunning in nature. Their rich hues subconsciously evoke feelings of courage, wisdom, and grandness.

This chapter presents to you this spectacular group of violet-spectrum colors in five color sections: violet, blue-violet, red-violet, purple, and fuchsia.

If you would like to work with one of these color families, go directly to its section. Once you have decided which color scheme to use, review its guidelines in Chapter Two. If you want to review other color hints, refer to Chapter One.

ROYAL VIOLET
AND ALL ITS GLORY

Violet is the darkest pure color on the color wheel. It is located at the bottom of the color wheel, halfway between magenta and turquoise. Its rich hues are displayed frequently in nature. Because violet is so dark in value, it is the pure color with the most tints. The tints range from blush white to many lavender, lilac, and light violet hues. There are few shades in its family, since it takes very few steps to move from pure violet to black. The subtle tones of violet can be seen at the right. Grayed dark violet produces eggplant and grape hues.

The Subtle Beauty of the Violet Monochromatic Color Scheme

Using only pure violet, along with its tints, tones, and shades for a monochromatic color scheme creates a sophisticated, beautiful color scheme.

Dutch Rose
Monochromatic

The hues on this page can be used monochromatically or they may be used in any other color scheme that includes violet.

Tints (violet + white)

Shades (violet + black)

Tones (pure violet + gray)

Tones (light violet + gray)

Tones (dark violet + gray)

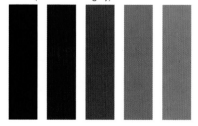

Violet and Its Complement

Violet and its complementary partner yellow form a partnership that naturally mimics the effect of sunlight through deep shadows. This physical relationship can be used to your advantage when working with these complements. A fabric selection is shown on page 38. Spinning Around the Block on page 46 uses violet as yellow's complement.

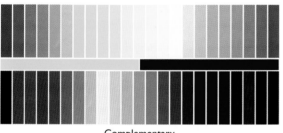

Complementary

Complementary

Dutch Rose
Complementary

Analogous Violet

Violet can be very beautiful in an analogous color scheme with three, five, or seven colors (see photo 64B). Although violet is usually in the center position, it can be positioned on either end of the analogous color range. Nancy's Fancy on page 105 uses violet analogously.

Analogous

Dutch Rose
Analogous

Analogous

Violet's Split-Complementary Color Scheme

The split-complementary color scheme is a glorious showcase for violet, since it combines its analogous neighbors with yellow. Spinning Around the Block on page 46 and Nancy's Fancy on page 105 use violet in a split-complementary color scheme.

Split-Complementary

Dutch Rose
Split-Complementary

Violet's Secondary Triadic Color Scheme

Violet, green, and orange are secondary colors; their combination is called a secondary triadic color scheme. A triadic fabric selection is shown on page 51. Violet is used in a triadic color plan in Stepping Stones on page 62.

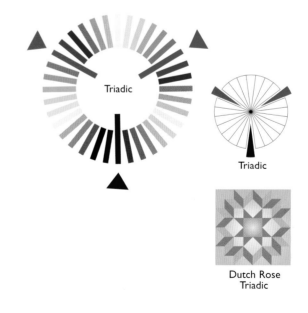

Triadic

Triadic

Dutch Rose
Triadic

VERY COOL BLUE-VIOLET

Blue-violet lies between violet and blue on the color wheel. Blue-violet is stunning, no matter whether you are looking at its tints, the pure hue, or its shades. Sunrises and sunsets frequently give us blue-violet skies, while hydrangeas, lobelia, and blueberries amaze us with their unusual blue-violet hues. This beautiful color family can be used to create sophisticated, calming designs.

Monochromatic Blue-Violet

Using blue-violet in a monochromatic color plan can result in a soothing, elegant design. It may take some time to gather a good collection of fabrics in a wide value range, since this is not a color that is available in abundance. However, collecting the fabrics should be fun. A fabric selection is shown below.

Blue-Violet Fabrics

Dutch Mill
Monochromatic

The hues on this page can be used monochromatically or they may be used in any other color scheme that includes blue-violet.

Tints (blue-violet + white)

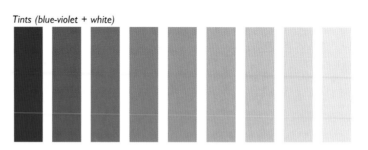

Shades (blue-violet + black)

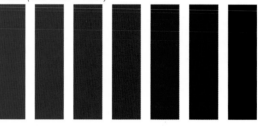

Tones (pure blue-violet + gray)

Tones (light blue-violet + gray)

Tones (dark blue-violet + gray)

Complementary Blue-Violet

We frequently see the natural color combination of blue-violet and its complement golden-yellow in sunsets. Dutch Mill on page 104 and Delectable Mountains on page 47 can be seen in a complementary color scheme.

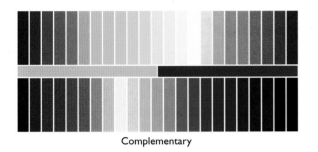

Complementary

Complementary

Dutch Mill
Complementary

Analogous Blue-Violet

There are many harmonic analogous possibilities for blue-violet and its analogous neighbors. The patterns Laurel Wreath on page 90 and Dutch Mill on page 104 show analogous color schemes using blue-violet.

Analogous

Dutch Mill
Analogous

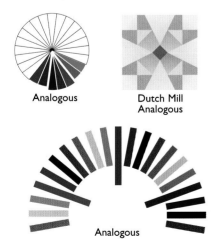

Analogous

Blue-Violet and Its Split-Complementary Combinations

Blue-violet works very well in a split-complementary color scheme because of the wonderful temperature shift it creates with golden-yellow. Dutch Mill on page 104 and Delectable Mountains on page 47 are shown in split-complementary color plans.

Split-Complementary

Dutch Mill
Split-Complementary

The Unexpected Triadic Partnership

The wonderfully unexpected triadic partners of blue-violet are orange-red and spring green. Their hues blend beautifully together. Dutch Mill on page 104 and Star Stretch on page 63 show blue-violet with its triadic partners.

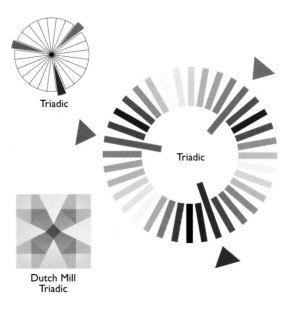

Triadic

Triadic

Dutch Mill
Triadic

RIOTOUS RED-VIOLET

Red-violet is very closely associated with both violet and purple, as it lies between them on the color wheel. It is slightly redder than violet and a bit cooler than purple. It is often a forgotten color, as purple and violet receive the most attention. In fact, many people mistakenly think red-violet is violet or purple. Nature uses red-violet frequently. Red-violet's tints are numerous, while its shades are few. Notice the beauty of the tones. Darkened red-violet creates a rich burgundy—almost a wine brown. The light hues create lovely lilac colors.

Monochromatic Red-Violet

If you love red-violet and have a variety of fabrics with a wide value scale, consider creating a monochromatic design. It should be magnificent!

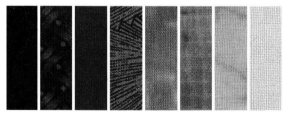

Red-Violet Fabrics

Golden Royalty
Monochromatic

The hues on this page can be used monochromatically or they may be used in any other color scheme that includes red-violet.

Tints (red-violet + white)

Shades (red-violet + black)

Tones (pure red-violet + gray)

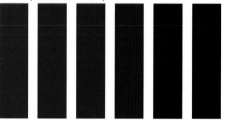

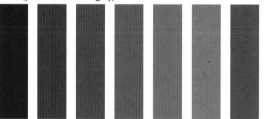

Tones (light red-violet + gray)

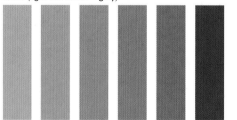

Tones (dark red-violet + gray)

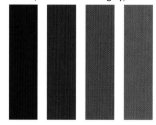

Red-Violet and Its Complement

Like other striking colors, red-violet looks absolutely wonderful with its opposing partner, chartreuse. They seemingly vibrate off each other. Any design should look smashing with this combination.

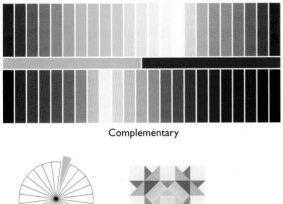

Complementary

Complementary

Golden Royalty
Complementary

Analogous Red-Violet

Red-violet and its harmonic neighbors make for a wonderful analogous color scheme. Red-violet is used analogously in Dutch Mill on page 104 and Nancy's Fancy on page 105.

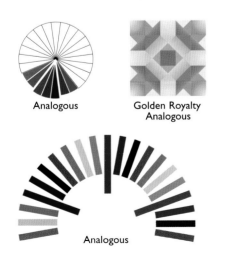

Analogous

Golden Royalty
Analogous

Analogous

Red-Violet and Its Beautiful Temperature Shift

Red-violet works beautifully in a split-complementary color plan along with vibrant chartreuse. You can change the mood considerably by having red-violet as chartreuse's complement and greens and yellows as the analogous group. A fabric selection is shown on page 45. Dutch Mill on page 104 and Nancy's Fancy on page 105 use red-violet in their split-complementary plans.

Split-Complementary

Golden Royalty
Split-Complementary

Red-Violet and Its Surprising Triadic Partners

Red-violet's triadic partners are yellow-orange and blue-green. They make a great combination. A triadic plan is used in Through the Looking Glass on page 129.

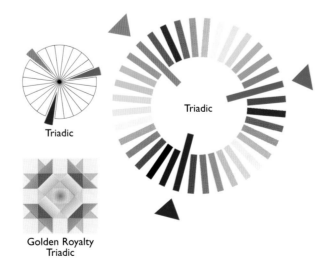

Triadic

Triadic

Golden Royalty
Triadic

VERY POPULAR PURPLE

Purple is a wonderfully warm, luminous color worthy of its popularity. It lies halfway between magenta and violet and thus has more red in its make-up than violet. Purple evokes strength and splendor. During important ceremonies and certain seasons of the church year, religious attire is often made from purple cloth.

Because purple is a relatively dark color, tints are numerous. Notice that the tints in purple's family are much warmer than violet's tints. Purple's small shade scale is filled with rich, luscious hues. Purple tones are beautiful and subtle. You will find forms of lilac and mauve in this family.

Monochromatic Purple

If you want to use only purple in your design, include pure purple and as many tints, shades, and tones as you wish.

Nancy's Fancy
Monochromatic

The hues on this page can be used monochromatically or they may be used in any other color scheme that includes purple.

Tints (purple + white)

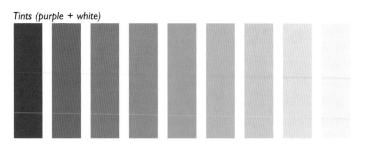

Shades (purple + black)

Tones (pure purple + gray)

Tones (light purple + gray)

Tones (dark purple + gray)

Purple's Stunning Complement —Yellow-Green

Purple's complement is yellow-green. They make a glorious partnership, as you can see by the hues here. Nancy's Fancy on page 105 shows this complementary plan. A selection of fabrics is shown at the right.

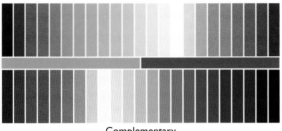

Complementary

An important note: If you are not certain whether you are working with purple, red-violet, or violet, give your fabric the afterimage test. For detailed information on finding an afterimage, see Chapter Two, page 26.

Purple and Its Analogous Possibilities

If you are a purple lover, consider using the analogous color scheme. All combinations are beautiful. One example is shown in Nancy's Fancy on page 105.

Analogous

Analogous

Nancy's Fancy
Complementary

Complementary

Nancy's Fancy
Analogous

Complementary
Purple and Yellow-Green

Purple with Its Beautiful Split-Complementary Combination

Using the split-complementary color scheme with purple is wonderful because the yellow-green temperature change is so striking. For variation you can make purple the complement that combines with yellow-green and its analogous hues. Split-complementary color plans are shown in Nancy's Fancy on page 105 and Celebration on page 32.

shown in Nancy's Fancy on page 105 and Celebration on page 32.

Split-
Complementary

Nancy's Fancy
Split-Complementary

Purple's Triadic Partnership

Purple has a gorgeous triadic partnership with aqua green and orange-yellow. Many hues you can use are shown here. This combination would make a great quilt! A fabric selection is shown at the right. Nancy's Fancy is shown with a triadic color plan on page 105.

Nancy's Fancy is shown with a triadic color plan on page 105.

Triadic

Triadic

Nancy's Fancy
Triadic

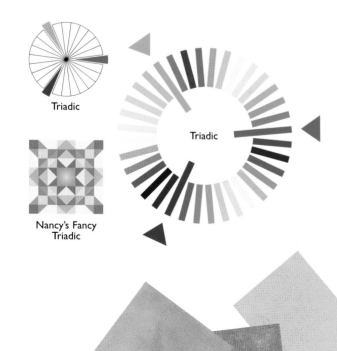

Triadic
Purple, Aqua Green,
and Orange-Yellow

FABULOUS FUCHSIA AND ITS COLORFUL OPPORTUNITIES

Fuchsia is a stunning color which lies between magenta and purple. It is relatively cool, beautifully clear, and filled with energy. Gardens vibrate with flowers strikingly colored with fuchsia. Fuchsia's tints are beautiful cool pinks in light and medium values. Fuchsia's shades are rich, vibrant hues of exquisite deep wine colorings. Fuchsia's tones are soft and subtle. The dark tones range from an exquisite burgundy wine to luscious wine brown. The very grayed pinks become mauve as they lose their identity.

The Sophisticated Fuchsia Monochromatic Color Scheme

Using fuchsia in a monochromatic color scheme can create a vibrant design. Its color range will offer a rich, dynamic statement.

Fly Away
Monochromatic

The hues on this page can be used monochromatically or they may be used in any other color scheme that includes fuchsia.

Tints (fuchsia + white)

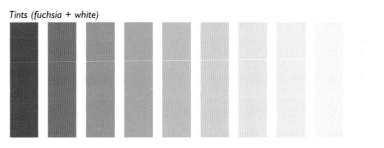

Shades (fuchsia + black)

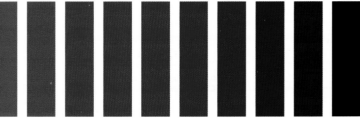

Tones (pure fuchsia + gray)

Tones (light fuchsia + gray)

Tones (dark fuchsia + gray)

Analogous
Fuchsia

Fuchsia's Beautiful Complementary Partner

Fuchsia looks stunning with spring green, its complementary partner. Star Stretch on page 63 uses a complementary color plan.

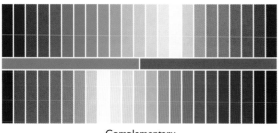

Complementary

Fly Away
Complementary

Complementary

Fuchsia's Analogous Opportunities

Fuchsia can be very pretty when combined with its neighbors. Besides having fuchsia as the middle color, you can position fuchsia on either end of the color range. Nancy's Fancy on page 105 uses the analogous color plan.

Analogous

Fly Away
Analogous

Analogous

Split-Complementary Fuchsia

Fuchsia and its neighbors magenta and purple are great colors to use with spring green, fuchsia's complement. Stretch your analogous range to five colors for more interest, if you wish. A fabric selection is shown at the right. Star Stretch, Nancy's Fancy, and Storm at Sea (nine-patch) on pages 63, 105, and 119 use the split-complementary color scheme.

Lovely Triadic Fuchsia

Aqua blue and golden-yellow are fuchsia's striking triadic partners. Delectable Mountains uses fuchsia in its triadic color scheme on page 47.

Fly Away
Split-Complementary

Split-Complementary

Split-Complementary
Fuchsia with Spring Green

Triadic

Triadic

Fly Away
Triadic

DUTCH MILL (5-patch pattern) in four different blue-violet color schemes

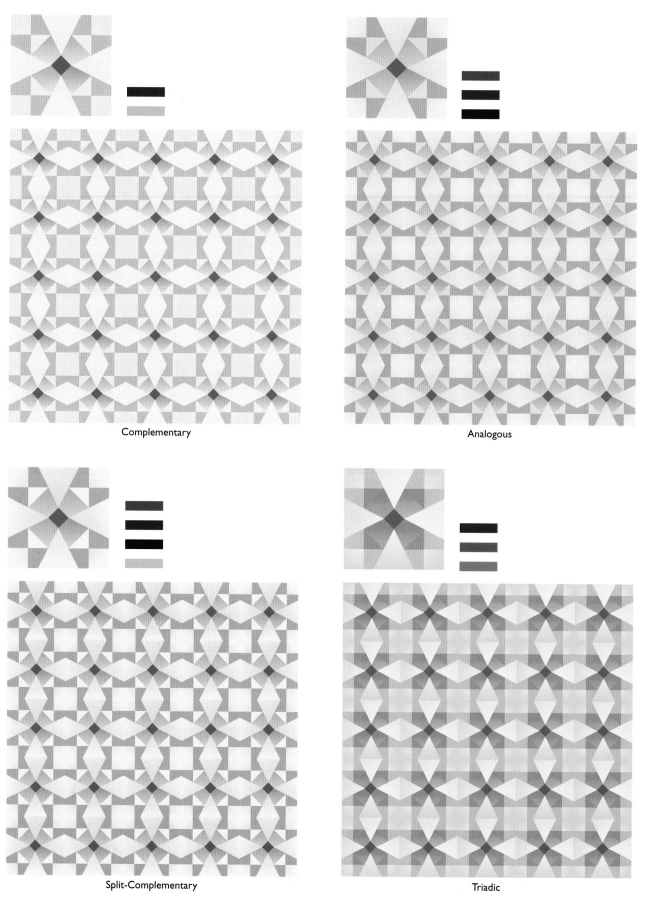

Complementary

Analogous

Split-Complementary

Triadic

NANCY'S FANCY

(four-patch pattern) in four different purple color schemes

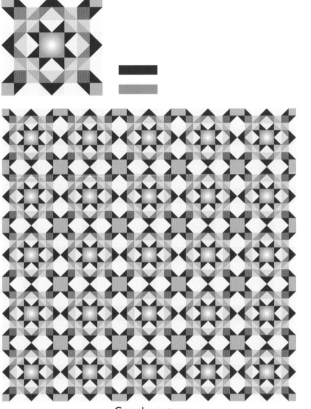

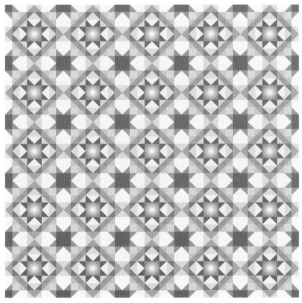

Complementary

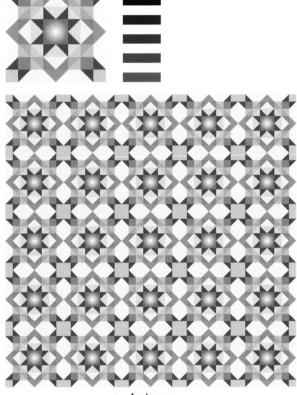

Analogous

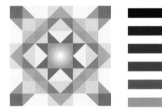

Split-Complementary

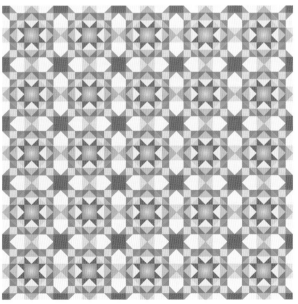

Triadic

chapter seven
RAMBUNCTIOUS REDS

red
orange-red
blue-red
magenta

The red spectrum is beautifully vibrant and exciting. It moves from warm orange-reds to red, and then on to cool blue-reds and magenta. No doubt you will find a color in this range that fits your personality. This chapter is divided into four color sections: red, orange-red, blue-red, and magenta. Once you have decided which red color you wish to use, select your preferred color scheme. Then go to Chapter Two for color plan guidelines. If you want to learn about color scales, value, or color temperature, refer to Chapter One. Have fun working with some of the warmest colors on earth.

RAMBUNCTIOUS RED AND ITS FAMILY

Red elicits excitement, intensity, and fervor. Anger, passion, love, bravery, blood, strength, life, and fire are all tightly bound to the emotional, mental, and physical images of the red color family.

Red affects the eye's retina more than any other color. Because of this, red can raise blood pressure, quicken the pulse, and increase the breathing rate and muscle activity.

Pure red is an exciting color to use. Red's tints are luscious, lovely pinky corals. When red is blackened, it changes from the pure red to beautiful reddish rust, and then to a rich brown. The tones are lovely. Tones include dusty corals, pinky grays, and mauve.

Monochromatic Red

If you want to work monochromatically, use tints, shades, and tones along with pure red.

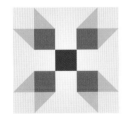

Butterfly at the Crossroads
Monochromatic

The hues on this page can be used monochromatically or they may be used in any other color scheme that includes red.

Tints (red + white)

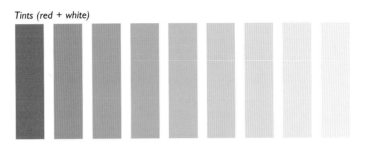

Shades (red + black)

Tones (pure red + gray)

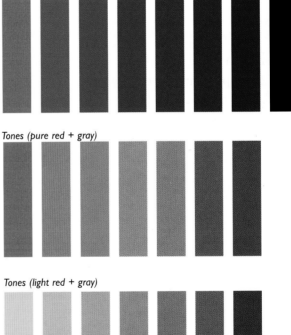

Tones (light red + gray)

Tones (dark red + gray)

Red and Its Complement Aqua Green

Red's complementary partner is aqua green. These two colors work gloriously together. A fabric selection is shown at the right. If you use green instead of aqua green for red's complementary companion, the beauty of your design is compromised, because green is not red's natural partner. As you can see, green does not lie opposite red on the color wheel.

Complementary

Not Complementary

Butterfly at the Crossroads
Complementary

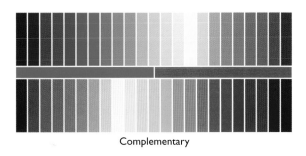

Complementary

Analogous Red

You can create a visually harmonic design by using red and its close neighboring color families. Use three, five, or seven color families in your analogous design. Generally, red will be your center color, but you can also place it on either end of your color span too.

Analogous

Butterfly at the Crossroads
Analogous

Analogous

Complementary
Red and Aqua Green

Red's Split-Complementary Colors

Red is lovely in a split-complementary design. You can place it in the middle of three, five, or seven analogous hues. Its complement, aqua green, creates a wonderful temperature change. Likewise, red can become the complementary temperature-shifting color while aqua green and its neighbors form the analogous range.

Split-Complementary
Red with Aqua Green

Split-
Complementary

Butterfly at the Crossroads
Split-Complementary

Red's Triadic Partnership

The triadic partners with red are yellow-green and blue. Many beautiful hues can combine to make a very striking design. A fabric selection can be seen at the right.

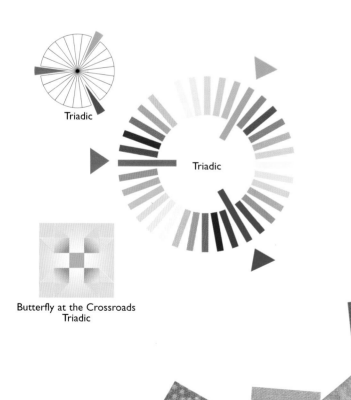

Triadic

Triadic

Butterfly at the Crossroads
Triadic

GLOWING ORANGE-RED AND ITS COLOR FAMILY

Pure orange-red, a color with slightly more yellow in its makeup than red, is beautifully rich and warm. It is the color of vine-ripened tomatoes, strawberries, oriental poppies, and dozens of other stunning flowers. The orange-red tints are a lovely blend between coral and peach. As orange-red is darkened with black, its hues turn into warm orange-red rusts and scrumptious orange-red browns. Orange-red's shade scale has exceptionally beautiful rusts and browns. The orange-red tones include salmon, as well as subtle wintry hues.

Monochromatic Orange-Red

If you would like to work solely with the dynamic orange-red family, select hues from the tint, shade, and tone scales, along with the pure color. A selection of fabrics can be seen below.

Orange-Red Fabrics

Bachelor's Puzzle
monochromatic

The hues on this page can be used monochromatically or they may be used in any other color scheme that includes orange-red.

Tints (orange-red + white)

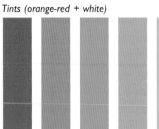

Shades (orange-red + black)

Tones (pure orange-red + gray)

Tones (light orange-red + gray)

Tones (dark orange-red + gray)

Orange-Red and Its Complement

The warmth of orange-red is beautifully cooled by the lovely aqua blue hues. Bachelor's Puzzle is shown in a complementary plan on page 118.

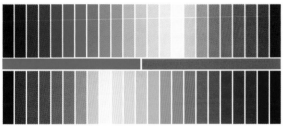

Complementary

Complementary

Bachelor's Puzzle
Complementary

Analogous Orange-Red

There are numerous analogous possibilities when using orange-red as your dominant color using three, five, or seven colors. You can position orange-red in the center or at either end of the range. The Bachelor's Puzzle pattern on page 118 shows this harmonious color scheme.

Analogous

Bachelor's Puzzle
Analogous

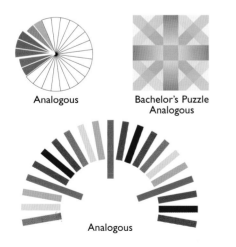

Analogous

Playing with Split-Complementary Colors

Orange-red and its analogous colors are beautiful together with complementary aqua blue providing the temperature shift. This combination is shown in Bachelor's Puzzle on page 118. For a different effect, orange-red can be used as the temperature-changing complementary color (page 88).

Split-
Complementary

Bachelor's Puzzle
Split-Complementary

Orange-Red's Triadic Partnership

Orange-red's triadic partners are spring green and blue-violet. These color families work beautifully together, as you can see in Bachelor's Puzzle on page 118.

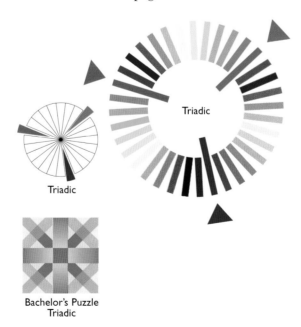

Triadic

Triadic

Bachelor's Puzzle
Triadic

BONNY BLUE-RED —A VERY COOL RED

If you prefer a slightly cool red, you may wish to work with luscious blue-red. Blue-red's tints are cool, beautiful pinks. The shades are very rich. Cranberry and maroon appear as black is added. The luscious tones have a hint of wine in them. Light-colored tones move from a slightly grayed pink to mauve.

Monochromatic Blue-Red

As you can see, the tints, shades, and tones of blue-red would be wonderful in a monochromatic plan.

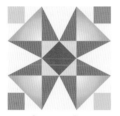

Storm at Sea
Monochromatic

The hues on this page can be used monochromatically or they may be used in any other color scheme that includes blue-red.

Tints (blue-red + white)

Shades (blue-red + black)

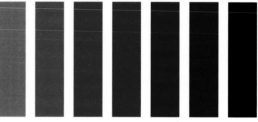

Tones (pure blue-red + gray)

Tones (light blue-red + gray)

Tones (dark blue-red + gray)

Blue-Red's Complementary Partner

Blue-red and its complementary partner blue-green create a beautiful combination. Storm at Sea in a complementary plan is shown on page 119. A lovely fabric selection is shown at the right.

Complementary

Storm at Sea Complementary

Complementary

Complementary Blue-Red with Blue-Green

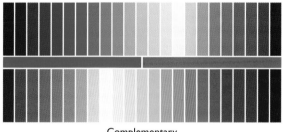

Blue-Red's Analogous Combinations

You can work with three, five, or seven analogous colors with blue-red in the center position. Also, you can make blue-red an outer color in the range. The nine-patch Storm at Sea on page 119 is shown in an analogous plan.

Analogous

Storm at Sea Complementary

Analogous

Blue-Red's Split-Complementary Possibilities

The smallest split-complementary color combination uses blue-red, magenta, red, and complementary blue-green. Storm at Sea (nine-patch) can be seen in a split-complementary plan on page 119.

Split-
Complementary

Storm at Sea
Split-Complementary

Blue-Red's Intriguing Triadic Partners

Blue-red creates wonderful color play with its two triadic partners chartreuse and cerulean blue (sky blue). Storm at Sea is shown in a triadic plan on page 119. A fabric selection can be seen on the right.

Triadic

Triadic

Storm at Sea
Triadic

MAGNIFICENT MAGENTA

Besides being a glorious color, magenta is one of the three primary colors on the Ives Color Wheel (page 11). Pure magenta is strong and refreshing. Magenta's tints are cool pinks and its shades are gloriously rich. When magenta hues are toned, their subtle coloring changes to lovely mauves and breathtaking, rich wine hues.

Monochromatic Magenta

If you wish to use only the magenta family in your design, use it with its tints, shades, and tones.

Celebration
Monochromatic

The hues on this page can be used monochromatically or they may be used in any other color scheme that includes magenta.

Tints (magenta + white)

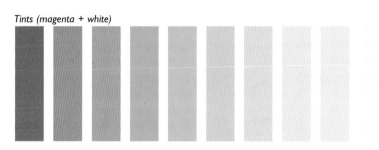

Shades (magenta + black)

Tones (pure magenta + gray)

Tones (light magenta + gray)

Tones (dark magenta + gray)

Magenta and Its Complement Green

Magenta looks fabulous with green, its complement. These colors can create a glorious design (page 62). A fabric selection can be seen on page 50.

Celebration
Complementary

Complementary

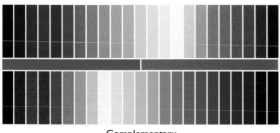

Complementary

Magenta and Its Analogous Opportunities

Magenta and its neighboring colors can create quite a dynamic combination. Generally magenta would be in the center position, but you can slide it to one of the outer edges of the color range too. A fabric selection is shown on the right.

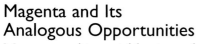

Analogous

Celebration
Analogous

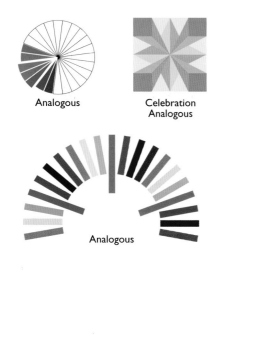

Analogous

Analogous
Magenta

Playing with the Split-Complementary Possibilities

Magenta used in a design with its analogous hues and its complement, green, can be quite stunning. A striking variation would use magenta as the complement with green and its analogous colors playing opposite. A split-complementary fabric selection is shown at the right.

Magenta's Triadic Partnership

Magenta and the other two primary colors, yellow and turquoise, create the popular primary triadic color scheme. An example of magenta in a triadic color plan can be seen on page 46 and in quilt photo 68C.

Triadic

Triadic

Celebration
Split-Complementary

Split-Complementary

Celebration
Triadic

Split-Complementary
Magenta with Green

BACHELOR'S PUZZLE

(five-patch pattern) in four different orange-red color schemes

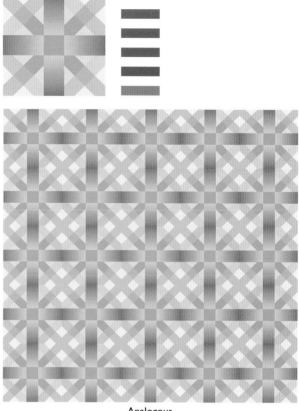

Complementary

Analogous

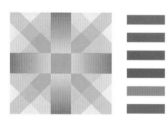

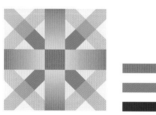

Split-Complementary

Triadic

STORM AT SEA (nine-patch pattern) in four different blue-red color schemes

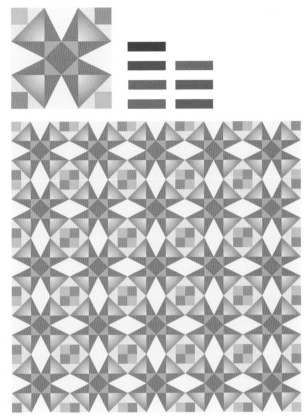

Complementary

Analogous

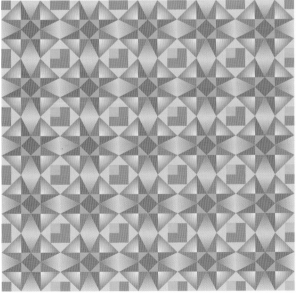

Split-Complementary

Triadic

chapter eight
OUTRAGEOUS ORANGES

orange
yellow-orange
orange-yellow

The orange color spectrum includes orange, yellow-orange, and orange-yellow. Pure orange is an outrageously beautiful color. Gently colored spring flowers, vibrant summer blooms, and magical autumnal hues use this warm color spectrum with marvelous effect. Sunsets paint the sky with streaks of vivid oranges that vibrantly dance across the sky. This chapter is divided into three color sections: orange, yellow-orange, and orange-yellow.

If you enjoy working within this color range, select one of these as your dominant color for your forthcoming project. Decide which color scheme you would like to use. For detailed information about each color scheme's characteristics and guidelines, go to Chapter Two. If you would like to review guidelines for color scales, values, intensity, or color temperature, turn to Chapter One.

OUTRAGEOUS ORANGE—ITS PERSONALITY AND FAMILY

Pure orange lies halfway between magenta and yellow on the color wheel. It is filled with energy and warmth. Family members include rust, brown, apricot, and salmon. Delicate or bold, the orange family holds an enticing beauty of its own.

Orange's Monochromatic Color Scheme

The orange family makes a stunning monochromatic quilt. A selection of fabrics is shown below.

Orange Fabrics

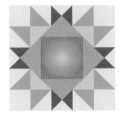

King David's Crown
Monochromatic

The hues on this page can be used monochromatically or they may be used in any other color scheme that includes orange.

Tints (orange + white)

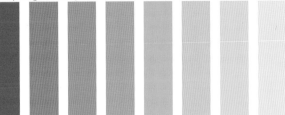

Shades (orange + black)

Tones (pure orange + gray)

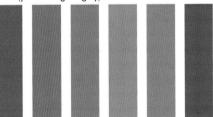

Tones (light orange + gray)

Tones (dark orange + gray)

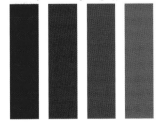

Complementary Oranges

Orange and turquoise elicit the extremes of hot and cold. Storm at Sea is colored in a complementary plan on page 89. A complementary fabric selection is shown on page 84. As you can see below, blue is not the complement to orange, as it does not lie opposite it on the color wheel.

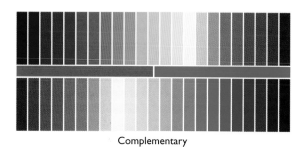

Complementary

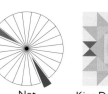

Complements   Not Complements   King David's Crown Complementary

Analogous Orange

Use orange analogously for a beautiful color blend. Bachelor's Puzzle and Through the Looking Glass on pages 118 and 129 use orange analogously.

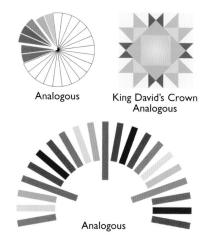

Analogous   King David's Crown Analogous

Analogous

Split-Complementary Oranges

Orange is beautiful in a split-complementary setting with turquoise creating a cool temperature shift. (See quilt photos 74A and 74B.) Generally a three- or five-color range is used, with orange in the middle position.

Split-Complementary   King David's Crown Split-Complementary

Orange's Triadic Color Scheme

Because orange lies halfway between magenta and yellow on the color wheel, it is considered a secondary color along with green and violet. These hues, with their color families and blends, create beautiful design opportunities. A fabric selection is shown on page 51. Orange is used with its triadic partners in Stepping Stones on page 62.

Triadic

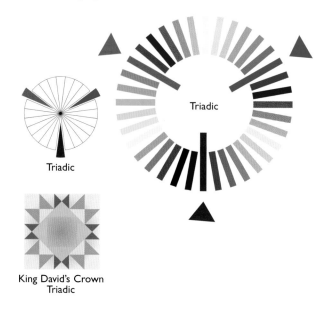

Triadic

King David's Crown Triadic

WARM, GLOWING YELLOW-ORANGE

Yellow-orange lies next to orange on the color wheel. It is a warmer color than orange due to its closer positioning to yellow. We frequently see yellow-orange in sunrises and sunsets. The gentle tints from the yellow-orange family can be seen at the right. These beautiful hues include the refreshing color of orange sherbet. Shades lean toward warm yellow rusts and warm browns. The yellow-orange tones vary depending on their values. However, all are muted.

Yellow-Orange and Its Monochromatic Color Schemes

If you want to create a design specifically with yellow-orange hues, include its tints, tones, and shades.

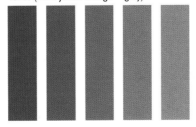

Through the
Looking Glass
Monochromatic

The hues on this page can be used monochromatically or they may be used in any other color scheme that includes yellow-orange.

Tints (yellow-orange + white)

Shades (yellow-orange + black)

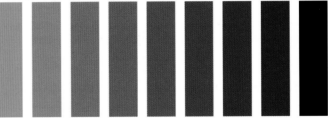

Tones (pure yellow-orange + gray)

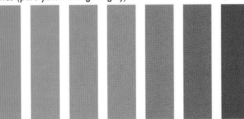

Tones (light yellow-orange + gray)

Tones (dark yellow-orange + gray)

Yellow-Orange and Its Lovely Complement

Yellow-orange has a beautiful complement—cerulean blue (sky blue). You often see this partnership in sunrises and sunsets. A complementary color scheme with Through the Looking Glass can be seen on page 129.

Through the
Looking Glass
Complementary

Complementary

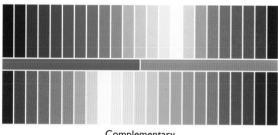

Complementary

Yellow-Orange and Its Analogous Possibilities

If you love warm colors, you will enjoy working with yellow-orange in an analogous setting. Place yellow-orange in the center position or have it as one of the outer colors on the range. Through the Looking Glass on page 129 is an example of yellow-orange in an analogous scheme. A fabric selection is shown at the right.

Analogous

Through the
Looking Glass
Analogous

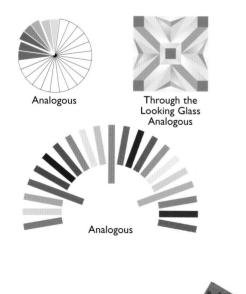

Analogous

Analogous
Yellow-Orange

Yellow-Orange and Its Split-Complementary Temperature Shift

Yellow-orange is beautifully enhanced in a split-complementary color scheme. Cerulean blue creates a soft coolness amidst yellow-orange and the other warm colors (see quilt photo 69B). If you want a cooler design, let yellow-orange be the complement to cerulean blue and its analogous neighbors. A fabric selection can be seen at the right. Through the Looking Glass is shown on page 129 in a split-complementary plan.

Through the
Looking Glass
Split-Complementary

Split-Complementary

Split Complimentary
Yellow-Orange with
Cerulean Blue

The Fantastic Yellow-Orange Triad

If you would like to create a design with an exceptional color combination, consider the yellow-orange, blue-green and red-violet triad. You can use the pure hues along with any of their tints, shades, and tones. Through the Looking Glass is colored in a triadic color plan on pages 129.

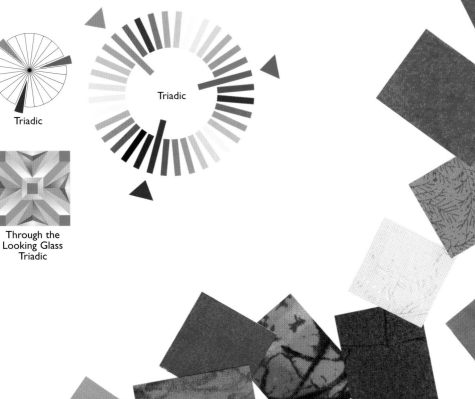

Triadic

Triadic

Through the
Looking Glass
Triadic

THE GENTLE HUES OF ORANGE-YELLOW

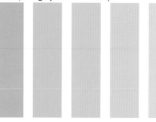

Orange-yellow is a warm, pure color which lies halfway between yellow and orange. It radiates a beautiful glow since it is so close to yellow. It is rather an important color in the color wheel, because its complement blue is so very popular. The hues of golden apricots and cantaloupes come from the orange-yellow family.

The soft orange-yellow tints can be seen at the right. These delicate hues are well suited for spring imagery. As black is added to orange-yellow, warm tans and beiges are created. As more black is added, warm yellow-browns appear. Toned orange-yellow hues are ever so subtle and slightly veiled.

Using Orange-Yellow in a Monochromatic Plan

If you want to work only with the orange-yellow family, you can combine the pure hue with many of its tints and shades.

Illusionary Star II
Monochromatic

The hues on this page can be used monochromatically or they may be used in any other color scheme that includes orange-yellow.

Tints (orange-yellow + white)

Shades (orange-yellow + black)

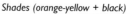

Tones (pure orange-yellow + gray)

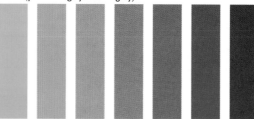

Tones (light orange-yellow + gray)

Tones (dark orange-yellow + gray)

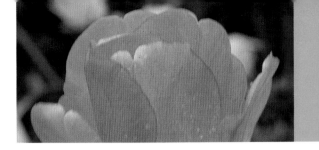

Orange-Yellow and Complementary Blue

Many people are surprised to learn that orange-yellow's opposing partner is blue. Sunsets and sunrises often display this complementary combination. It can be a very soothing partnership. A fabric selection is shown at the right. The pattern Laurel Wreath on page 90 shows this partnership.

Illusionary Star II
Complementary

Complementary

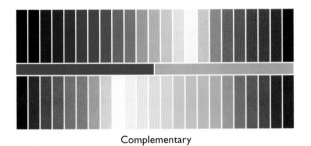

Complementary

Orange-Yellow and Its Many Analogous Possibilities

Orange-yellow and its warm analogous neighbors can provide lots of excitement in a design. Choose to work with three, five, or seven colors, using orange-yellow in the middle or outer position (see quilt photo 72A). You can see orange-yellow used analogously on page 129.

Analogous

Illusionary Star II
Analogous

Analogous

Complementary
Orange-Yellow and Blue

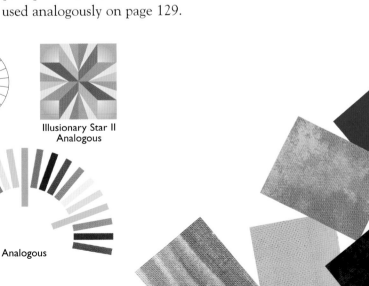

Orange-Yellow and Its Split-Complementary Options

The beautiful temperature shift in the split-complementary color scheme enhances orange-yellow greatly, as blue gives the design a sense of coolness (see quilt photo 7A). Generally orange-yellow is placed in the center position of your analogous color range. If you want a cooler design, consider placing orange-yellow in the complementary position, with blue and its analogous neighbors providing cool, refreshing contrast. A fabric selection can be seen at the right. Orange-yellow is the temperature-shifting color in Laurel Wreath on page 90.

Illusionary Star II
Split-Complementary

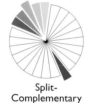

Split-Complementary

Split-Complementary
Orange-Yellow with Blue

Orange-Yellow's Triadic Partners

Orange-yellow's beautiful triadic partners are aqua-green and purple. They are stunning together. A fabric selection can be seen on page 100. Nancy's Fancy on page 105 uses this triadic partnership.

Triadic

Triadic

Illusionary Star II
Triadic

THROUGH THE LOOKING GLASS

(seven-patch pattern) in four different yellow-orange color schemes

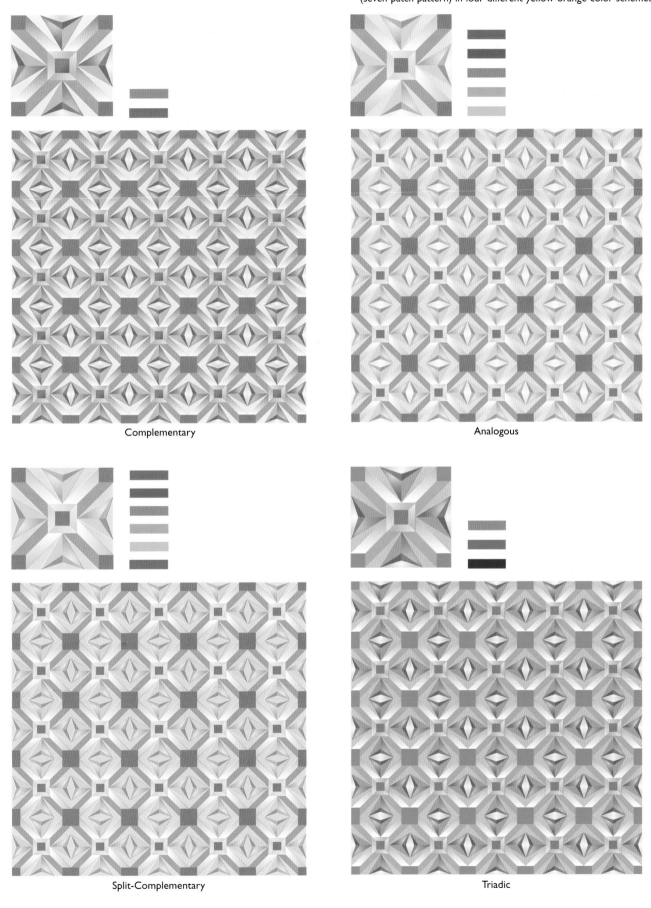

Complementary

Analogous

Split-Complementary

Triadic

130A GRANNY'S STAR, 1998, 68" × 92"
Susie Ernst, Petaluma, California

The subtle toned hues enhance this quilt's historic flavor. Darlene Zimmerman's *Aunt Maggie's Quilt* in *American Patchwork & Quilting®*, June 1997, inspired this lovely, nostalgic-looking quilt. Machine quilted by Lori Kelly. *(Photo: Ken Wagner)*

130B RED WILLOW STAR, 1998, 68" × 75"
Betty Colburn, Austin, Texas

Red Willow Star, a Broken Star quilt, exhibits luminosity with its clear-colored aqua shapes surrounded by toned hues. This contrast creates luminosity.
(Photo: Brenda Ladd)

130C THE SWAGMAN, 1993, 45" × 44"
Beth Miller, Kambah ACT, Australia

A reprint of a 1912 photo inspired *The Swagman*. The subtle, toned fabrics are in keeping with the quilt's mood.
(Photo: Andrew Sikorski)

130D LEANNE'S FOLLY, 1997, 85" × 100"
Leanne Vesecky, Baldwin City, Kansas

The subtle interplay of colors in Leanne's quilt creates transparency and a wonderful sense of visual vibration. The quilt was inspired by a Tennessee Star quilt in *Quilter's Newsletter Magazine®*.
(Photo: Ken Wagner)

131A NOVEMBER, 1998, 60" × 40"
Diana Voyer, Victoria,
British Columbia, Canada

November's wind and rain on Vancouver Island inspired this Snail's Trail pattern quilt. The subtle imagery reflects the sea and sky merging. The bits of yellow and orange relate to the brief, autumn days from the previous season.
(Photo: Ken Wagner)

131B IN EN UIT;
INSPIRATIE EN UITSTRALING
(In and out; Inspiration and Radiance),
1998, 57" × 57"
Marian Henstra, Aerdenhaut, The Netherlands.

Using the colorwash technique, Marian blended various colors from light to dark and dark to light, creating this subtly stunning design. The value changes create a lustrous effect.
(Photo: Gerard van Yperen)

131C A WALK IN WINTER: WHEELING
1939, 1998, 31" × 43"
Kathryn Vitek, Rockville, Maryland

This clever quilt was designed from family photos. It depicts Kathryn's mother, father, and herself. Unbelievably, this wintry quilt was made entirely of old neckties. Kathy hand-painted some neckties for the foreground snow.
(Photo: Mark Gulezian/QuickSilver)

chapter nine
IRRESISTIBLE ILLUSIONS

depth
luminosity
luster
shadows
highlights
transparency

Some of the most fascinating illusions to pique our imagination are presented in this chapter. Use illusions in traditional quilt settings, nature scenes, or any other designs. Whether you are working with blocks or appliqué designs, the illusion of depth enhances quilts. The impression of light created through color play can create depth, luminosity, luster, shadows, highlights, and transparency. These illusions are fun to use and amazingly easy to create. Select your favorite illusion, then follow the guidelines for creating it in your design. As you gain experience, choose other illusions to explore.

THE ILLUSION OF DEPTH

Creating Depth Through Atmospheric Perspective

As a scene unfolds before your eyes, you will see clearly the color and details of the foreground objects. As land elements and other objects recede into the distance, they become grayer in color (more toned), lighter in value, and less clear in detail (see photos at the right). This phenomenon is called atmospheric perspective, aerial perspective, or depth. Photos 5B and 6 show quilts that use atmospheric perspective.

If there is little value change between two land elements, such as mountains, it means these two elements are relatively close together (the first, second, and third hills in the top photo, e.g.). If there is strong value contrast between land elements, the distance between them is great (the third and fourth, fourth and fifth, and fifth and sixth hills in the top photo, e.g.). Therefore, if you want to create the impression of vast distances between elements or design layers, value differences must show clearly. If you want elements to appear close, keep the values similar.

Traditional Patterns and Atmospheric Perspective

If you want to create depth in a traditional design, select a block pattern that can visually read as having three or more layers (see blocks at the right). Innumerable patterns can be used.

Dancing Star

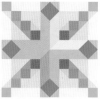

Beyond the Reef

Dove in the Window

Floating Jacks

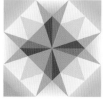

Vermont

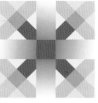

Bachelor's Puzzle

To create visual layers in your block pattern, select fabrics carefully. Colors must be more toned (grayed down), values must be lighter, and details must be more obscure as each layer moves back. Backgrounds work best when the fabrics' designs are mottled, blurred, solid-colored, or inconspicuously patterned. Backsides of fabrics often work well. If a clear hue or a pronounced print is used in a back layer, it will pop out or move forward visually. This will spoil the illusion of depth. Traditional quilts that show good depth can be seen in quilt photos 7A, 33B, and 68C.

Creating Depth by Overlapping

The overlapping of objects often creates the illusion of close-up dimensionality. Whenever an object or shape is placed on another, we assume the top object is closer than the lower one. The flowers in the photos illustrate how overlapping creates close-up dimensionality. Quilts using this form of dimensionality are shown in quilt photos 33A, 35A, 68C, and 130C. Also, overlapping objects is a common way to create dimensionality in the distance. In a picture or scene, overlapping enhances the dimensional effect (see quilt photos 67C, 72A, 131C, and 141B, and photos at the right).

Reducing Size to Create Depth

The illusion of depth is accentuated when objects become smaller as they move away from the foreground. Using lighter and grayer fabrics with little or no strong patterning can enhance depth further. Both picture and geometric designs can use this visual technique (see photos 70A and 141B).

As objects move away from the forground, they become smaller.

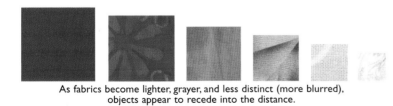

As fabrics become lighter, grayer, and less distinct (more blurred), objects appear to recede into the distance.

As objects move away from the foreground, they appear smaller.

Enhancing Depth Through Pattern and Textural Contrasts

Depth can be enhanced by contrasting textures. In nature, strongly colored objects or dark elements appear closer to us than grayed, muted colors or blurred images. In fabric, precisely printed, strong, or colorful designs attract our eyes easily. Therefore, they are most appropriate for a foreground. Mottled, blurred, or unclear designs tend to recede. Combining precisely printed, strong, or colorful patterning with blurred patterning creates a spatial difference between the two contrasts (see fabrics at right). (See quilt photos 65A, 67D, 68C, 73A, and 131A.)

CREATING THE ILLUSION OF LUMINOSITY

The sun, candlelight, and electric lights generate their own light sources. This glowing effect is called luminosity. Anything that glows or appears to glow is luminous. Sunrises and sunsets provide us with daily examples of luminosity. You can create luminosity in quilts, regardless of technique or design style (see photos 5B, 67A, 68C, and 131A).

Usually luminosity is created with pure colors, tints, or slightly shaded hues. These clear colors are then surrounded by toned hues. The surrounding grayness accentuates the clearness of the pure, tinted, or shaded hues, thus creating a luminous effect. Sometimes this grayness is very subtle as it surrounds the clear hues. At other times, the tonal contrast is quite pronounced.

If you do not have clear colors for your design's luminous area, use slightly toned hues as a substitute. Make certain the glowing area's surrounding hues are noticeably grayer in comparison. If a tonal (grayed) contrast cannot be seen, the luminous illusion will not appear. In Glowing Pineapples and Fortissimo in Plum (photos 141D and 143) the glowing areas are created with toned fabrics. However, the surrounding fabrics are considerably more toned; thus, luminosity appears. Also, make certain the luminous area is small compared to the total surface design. If it is too large, the illusion is lost. Purchase fabrics that appear luminous, or make your own luminous fabric with narrow strips or small fabric pieces.

Strongly patterned fabrics advance in a design while fabrics with blurred patterning tend to recede.

Create luminosity by surrounding clean, clear-colored fabrics with toned fabrics.

Using Luminosity in Traditional Patterns

Almost any traditional pattern can be enhanced by luminousity. Luminosity can be used within each block pattern, or you can create an overall luminous area. If you want to create luminosity within each block, select a pattern that has one or more shapes that will readily appear luminous when the colors are effectively applied (see blocks below).

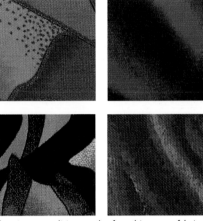

Luminous qualities can be found in some fabrics.

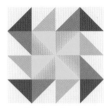

Yankee Puzzle

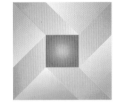

Formal Garden

Blazing Star

If you want to use luminosity as an overall background effect, work from a design wall. Position the clear background fabrics where you wish the luminous effect to appear. It can be in the quilt's center, at an outside edge, or wherever you choose. Place the remaining fabrics in the background, working from the least toned to very toned hues.

Luminosity moves from center outward in Star Trek.

Luminosity can move within the surface of the design.

CREATING THE ILLUSION OF LUSTER

A reflection made from a luminous object is called luster. Luster is quite common in nature. Sunlight falling on water creates luster. The moon's reflection on water or snow creates luster. Luster is created through value change. The light areas create the appearance of the reflected light. Luster is soft and subtle when there is very little value change between the lightest and darkest hues. If color values are strongly contrasted, the luster can be quite dramatic. Moving from a blush tint to a dark shade within a small area creates the most intense luster. Photos 1, 34A, 68B, 68C, 70C, 71A, 71C, 74B, 131B, and 141C show quilts which use luster in their designs.

Luster in the Foreground

You can create luster in hundreds of traditional blocks with a little imagination. Vertical, horizontal, and diagonal design bands are great places to incorporate luster. Making small value changes in your fabrics—moving from light to dark—is the key to creating luster within a shape or an area. Many fabrics already have value change in their designs, so you can use those to your benefit. Also, you can create your own lustrous fabric by sewing fabric strips with different value-change combinations (such as light to medium or medium to dark). Once you have made a variety of lustrous strip sets, you can cut the fabric for your design.

Mexican Cross

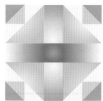

Duck and Ducklings

Luster can be created by combining fabrics that have progressive value changes.

Placing Luster in a Block's Background

You can strategically place luster within your block's background. A very basic pattern, such as Spinning Around the Block, Pinwheel, or Fly Away works well.

Pinwheel

Spinning Around the Block

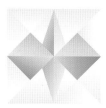

Fly Away

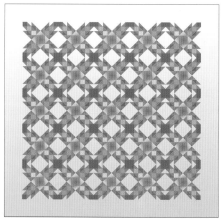

Lustrous background treatments can be created by changing values in a quilt's background (Woven Star).

Making a Lustrous Background

For exceptional drama, you may want to create a lustrous background with the foreground design appearing to float above it. To do this, subtly change the values of your background as you move from one area to another (at right). The lightest area can be in the center, at the edges, at the bottom, at the top, in one of the corners, or wherever you would like it.

CREATING THE ILLUSIONS OF SHADOWS AND HIGHLIGHTS

Shadows and highlights are marvelous illusions to incorporate in your designs. The results can be breathtaking, if you give care to color choices. Observe how colors change on flowers, snow, grass, and sand as shadows are formed. Also observe how strong sunlight creates highlights on flowers, leaves, trees, and other objects. Having a color wheel in front of you will make it much easier for you to select your colors and fabrics for your highlights or shadows.

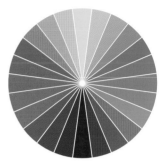

Creating Shadows

A shadow is created when an object stops light rays from continuing on their intended path. This blockage diminishes light and thus casts a shadow. It's surprising to realize that in nature shadows are not colored gray or black. Instead, shadow coloring moves toward violet, the darkest and lowest color on the color wheel. Specifically, an object's shaded color lies somewhere between the object's original color and violet. Examples of blocks with shading are shown below.

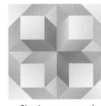
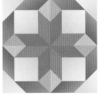

| Shadows created with shades (Beyond the Reef). | Shadows created with tones (Beyond the Reef). | Shadows created with shades (Rolling Star). | Shadows created with tones (Rolling Star). |

Besides moving toward violet, a shadow's color must be more shaded (blackened) or more toned (grayed) than the object's original color. There are multitudes of hues you can use for any color's shadow. Your choice will depend on how deep you want your shadow (how far it moves toward violet) and how toned or shaded it will be. If you want a slight shadow, move one or two steps downward from the original color along the color wheel. In addition to this color change, select a fabric that is darker or grayer than the original color. If you want a deeper shadow, drop to a lower color on the color wheel and make the color considerably more shaded or toned. A selection of colors and a few of their shadow options are shown on page 138. If your original color is very dark, then its shadow will be quite deep.

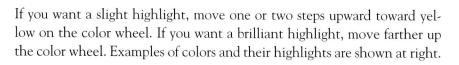

Golden-Yellow in light, medium, and dark shadows

Spring green in light, medium, and dark shadows

Shaded or toned colors have darker hues for shadows

Creating Highlights

A highlight is an area that is strongly filled with light. Extreme sunlight causes objects to appear as if they are drenched with sunny warmth. This flooding of sunlight on an object can be subtle or very intense. To create a highlight in a design, use a color for the highlighted object that has more yellow in its makeup than its original color. Consequently, move your highlighted color upward on the color wheel—heading toward yellow. In addition, the highlight should be more pure than the original color in order to look realistic.

If you want a slight highlight, move one or two steps upward toward yellow on the color wheel. If you want a brilliant highlight, move farther up the color wheel. Examples of colors and their highlights are shown at right.

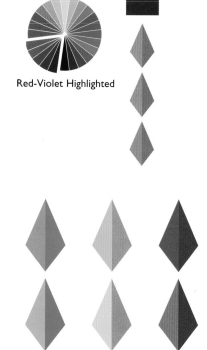

Red-Violet Highlighted

Other Hues Highlighted

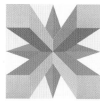

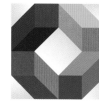
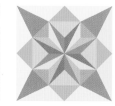

Illusionary Star

Spinning Around the Block

Bachelor's Puzzle

Wedding Ring

Using Highlights and Shadows in Your Designs

When creating a nature scene, try to incorporate highlights and shadows whenever possible. Study your original photograph to see where the highlights and shadows are placed. Imitate what you see as closely as possible. If you are using a design that does not show highlights or shadows, try creating your own lighting effects. You can make your design more realistic—and more interesting—if you do. Use fabrics that effectively create the illusion of highlights or shadows (see right) or create your own fabric combinations.

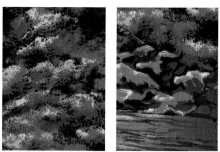

Some fabrics can be used to create the illusion of shadows or highlights.

CREATING THE ILLUSION OF TRANSPARENCY

A transparent object is one you can see through. An opaque object cannot be seen through.

Transparency appears when an area or shape seemingly lies transparently on top of either another transparent object or an opaque area or shape. Sometimes a transparency illusion is created quite by accident. Sometimes a fabric provides its own transparent effect (see right). You can also make your own transparency by careful placement of fabrics and colors.

Transparency is created with three colors—two *parent* colors and the transparent *offspring* color. Generally, one parent color appears transparent while the other parent color appears opaque. The selected offspring hue determines the parents' roles. If the offspring color is more like parent A, parent A will appear to transparently lie on top of parent B. If the offspring is more like parent B, parent B will assume the transparent role. If the offspring color is midway between both parents in color and value, both colors can appear transparent.

Fabrics showing transparency

Both colors are opaque; no transparency is present.

Yellow is transparent; green and rose are opaque.

Green and rose are transparent; yellow is opaque.

The offspring color is midway between the two parent colors.
Either color can appear transparent.

Working with Transparency

To create realistic transparency, have a color wheel beside you (see page 11 or 137). Select your parent colors. Blend these colors with pencils, crayons, or paints to find a transparent option.

Transparency combinations with parent colors from the same color families.

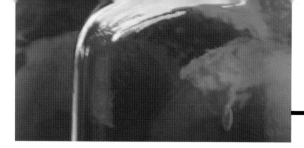

It is easy to create transparency using two colors that are in close proximity on the color wheel or from the same family. The overlapped offspring color will be a hue lying between the two on the color wheel—although the value and color scale may be different. The parent color closest to the offspring hue will appear transparent.

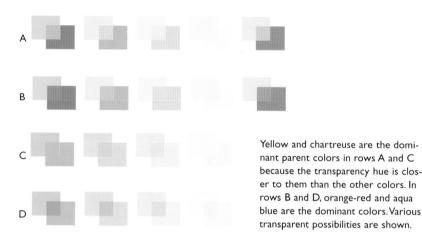

Yellow and chartreuse are the dominant parent colors in rows A and C because the transparency hue is closer to them than the other colors. In rows B and D, orange-red and aqua blue are the dominant colors. Various transparent possibilities are shown.

If you want to use transparency with your favorite color and its complement, play with your pencils, crayons, or paints to establish the transparent color. Tones are created when complements are mixed, so these transparent blends can be difficult to discern.

Transparency is more difficult to create when colors are used that are not closely related. Use your color pencils, crayons, or paints to find transparent possibilities. Usually color combinations far from each other on the color wheel will appear veiled, muddy, or toned. A selection of unrelated color partners that show transparency is shown at right.

Using Transparency with Traditional Patterns

Many traditional patterns can be greatly enhanced by incorporating transparency. Select patterns that have the possibility of two parent colors coming together to create an offspring transparent color. A selection of patterns are shown at the right.

Have a great time playing with illusions!

Magenta is the dominant transparent color.

Both parent colors can appear transparent, since the middle hue is halfway between magenta and green in hue and value.

Green is the dominant transparent color.

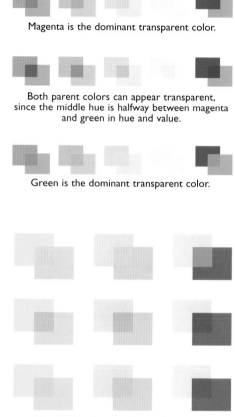

Unrelated colors can be used to create transparency. The transparent hues are usually very muddy or toned.

Around the Corner

North Dakota

Barbara Bannister's Transparent Star

Golden Royalty

141A FUCHSIA SERPENTINE, 1997, 45" x 45"
Reynola Pakusich, Bellingham, Washington

The warm-colored serpentine appears as if it is floating above the cool hues. Many colors appear transparent. Karen Stone's Pieced Arc pattern and Becky Olson's setting arrangement were used for this quilt.
(Photo: Louise Harris)

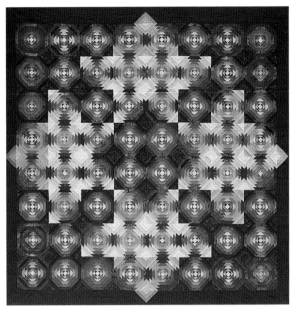

141C MAUI PINEAPPLE, 1997, 105" x 112"
Jane Loeffler, Pakalani, Hawaii

Maui Pineapple is an excellent example of how warm colors advance while cool hues recede. Its coloring makes *Maui Pineapple* appear as if there are several layers in the design.
(Photo: Ken Wagner)

141B FOLLOW THE YELLOW BRICK ROAD, 1995, 27" x 40"
Karen G. Harmony, Vida, Oregon

This fairy-tale quilt's imagery is quite striking with its combination of pure hues, tints, and shades. It was created using Joen Wolfrom's curved-piecing technique.
(Photo: Ken Wagner)

141D GLOWING PINEAPPLE, 1983, 46" x 54"
Diane Basch, Redmond, Washington

This traditional Pineapple Log Cabin design is an excellent example of luminosity. The toned fabrics around the clearer hues cause the latter colors to glow.
(Photo: Ken Wagner)

BIBLIOGRAPHY

Wolfrom, Joen. *The Magical Effects of Color,*
    California: C&T Publishing, 1992.

INDEX

afterimage 26
analogous colors 27-28, 32, 47, 62, 63,
    89, 90, 104, 105, 118, 119, 129
Basch, Daine 141
black 13, 16, 17
blue 13, 25, 26, 53, 77-90, 109, 127, 128
blue, cerulean 45, 81-82, 114, 124, 125
blue, aqua 42, 86-88, 111
blue, turquoise 25, 29, 31, 39, 83-85,
    117, 122
Boyd, Sandy 72, 73
brown 13, 14
Carels, Madelon 75
Carl, Anneliese 33
chartreuse 13, 28, 43-45, 82, 97, 114
Claridge, Clare 72
Colburn, Betty 130
Collet, Iek 34
color dominance 9, 10, 12, 14, 15, 21,
    25, 29, 30, 32
color families 10, 12, 22, 23, 26, 29, 31
color and nature 8-15, 22-24, 27-28, 31
color scales 9, 10, 21, 25
color schemes (plans) 22-31, 32, 46, 47,
    62, 63, 89, 90, 104, 105, 118, 119, 129
color temperature 20, 28-29
color wheel 10, 11, 24
complementary colors 24-26, 32, 47, 62,
    63, 89, 90, 104, 105, 118, 119, 129
Corry, Sandy 66, 72
Courtice, Helen 7
depth 132-134
Duffield, Sandy 72
Dyer, Joan 33
Eastmond, Elizabeth 64
Ernst, Susie 130
Evans, Noelle 64
Fallert, Caryl Bryer 68
Frovarp, Jackie 71
fuchsia 16, 42, 55, 56, 88, 101-103
Gilbert, Beth P. 74
Ginn, Martha W. 34, 70
gray 15, 16, 18

green 30, 48-63, 93, 116, 117, 122
green, aqua 16, 60-61, 100, 103, 108,
    109, 128
green, blue- 57-59, 97, 113, 114, 125
green, spring 54-56, 95, 102, 103, 111, 138
green, yellow- 17, 25, 28, 52-53, 80, 99,
    100, 109
Greenberg, Lesly-Claire 65
Harmony, Karen G. 141
Henstra, Marian 131
highlights 138
intensity 8, 10, 16-17, 23, 27
Ives color wheel 10, 11
Jenson, Ann 64
King, Sylvia I. 65
Lettau, Kay 75
Loeffler, Jane 141
luminosity 134-135
luster 135-136
Magee, Gwendolyn A. 69
magenta 29, 31, 32, 39, 50, 51, 85,
    115-117
Matthews, Dana 69
McFarland, Charlotte 67
MacWilliam, Irene 71
Martin, Elaine 76
Miller, Beth 71, 130
monochromatic color 22-24, 32
Nelson, Nancy A. 76
orange 14, 25, 30, 51, 84, 85, 93,
    120-129
orange, yellow- 14, 59, 82, 97, 123-125
Pakusich, Reynola 74, 141
Perkins, Patrice 75
perspective 132-133
primary colors 10, 11
pure colors 10
purple 23, 25, 29, 53, 61, 98-100, 128
red 13, 17, 53, 61, 80, 106-119, 138
red, blue- 20, 45, 58, 59, 82, 112-114
red, orange- 20, 56, 87, 88, 95, 110-111
Remick, Helen 70
Rhodes, Kaye 69, 76

Ropp, Gayle P. 1
Rowland, Carol 35
Sawada, Junko 7
scale, color 10-20, 21
scale, value 17-19
Schneider, Barbara 65, 75
Schutte, Paul 35
secondary colors 10, 11
shades 13-14
shadows 137-138
Sherman, Nellouise S. 70
split-complementary colors 28-29, 32, 47,
    62, 63, 89, 90, 104, 105, 118, 119, 129
temperature 20
tertiary colors 10
tints 10, 12
Tinling, Bonny 21
tones 15-16
transparency 139-140
triadic colors 29-31, 32, 47, 62, 63, 89,
    90, 104, 105, 118, 119, 129
turquoise 25, 29, 31, 39, 83-85, 117, 122
Underwood, Lynn 67
value 17-19
Vesecky, Leanne 130
violet 12, 25, 29, 30, 38, 39, 51,
    91-105, 122
violet, blue- 20, 41, 42, 56, 94-95, 111
violet, red- 44, 45, 59, 96-97, 125
Vitek, Kathryn 131
Voyer, Diana 66, 73, 131
Waters, Mariya A. 66, 74
Webb, Carol 34
Wells, Jean 33, 35
white 10, 11, 16, 17
Willey, Kit 68
Wolfrom, Joen 4, 5, 6, 76, 143
yellow 12, 13, 25, 28, 29, 31, 36-47,
    85, 93, 117
yellow, golden- 13, 14, 28, 40-42, 88,
    95, 103, 138
yellow, orange- 13, 14, 25, 28, 61, 79,
    80, 100, 126-128

143 FORTISSIMO IN PLUM, 1985, 60" x 36"
Joen Wolfrom, Fox Island, Washington

ABOUT THE AUTHOR

Joen began quiltmaking in 1974 after she left her career in the educational field to become a homemaker. Her interest in color and design surfaced in the early 1980s. Joen has taught and lectured in the quilting field, both nationally and internationally, since 1984. Her work is included in collections throughout the world. She is the author of five previously published books: *Make Any Block Any Size*; *Patchwork Persuasion*; *The Visual Dance*; *The Magical Effects of Color*; and *Landscapes & Illusions*.

Joen's leisure interests include gardening, antiquing, and reading. When not traveling, Joen enjoys life with her children and husband at her family's private home on a small island in Washington State.

Inquiries about workshop and lecture bookings and other correspondence may be sent directly to Joen Wolfrom at 104 Bon Bluff, Fox Island, Washington 98333. Requests for a current teaching schedule may be sent to the same address (include a large self-addressed, stamped envelope). Her homepage may be visited at http://www.mplx.com/joenwolfrom.

Other Fine Books From C&T Publishing:

15 Two-Block Quilts: Unlock the Secrets of Secondary Patterns, Claudia Olson

All About Quilting from A to Z, From the Editors and Contributors of Quilter's Newsletter Magazine and Quiltmaker Magazine

Along the Garden Path: More Quilters and Their Gardens, Jean Wells & Valori Wells

America from the Heart: Quilters Remember September 11, 2001, Karey Bresenhan

Art of Machine Piecing, The: How to Achieve Quality Workmanship Through a Colorful Journey, Sally Collins

Color from the Heart: Seven Great Ways to Make Quilts with Colors You Love, Gai Perry

Cotton Candy Quilts: Using Feed Sacks, Vintage, and Reproduction Fabrics, Mary Mashuta

Create Your Own Quilt Labels!, Kim Churbuck

Curves in Motion: Quilt Designs & Techniques, Judy Dales

Cut-Loose Quilts: Stack, Slice, Switch, and Sew, Jan Mullen

Do-It-Yourself Framed Quilts: Fast, Fun & Easy Projects, Gai Perry

Easy Pieces: Creative Color Play with Two Simple Quilt Blocks, Margaret Miller

Enchanted Views: Quilts Inspired by Wrought-Iron Designs, Dilys Fronks

Fantastic Fabric Folding: Innovative Quilting Projects, Rebecca Wat

Four Seasons in Flannel: 23 Projects—Quilts & More, Jean Wells & Lawry Thorn

Freddy's House: Brilliant Color in Quilts, Freddy Moran

Garden-Inspired Quilts: Design Journals for 12 Quilt Projects, Jean & Valori Wells

Ghost Layers and Color Washes: Three Steps to Spectacular Quilts, Katie Pasquini Masopust

Hidden Block Quilts: • *Discover New Blocks Inside Traditional Favorites* • *13 Quilt Settings* • *Instructions for 76 Blocks*, Lerlene Nevaril

Imagery on Fabric, Second Edition: A Complete Surface Design Handbook, Jean Ray Laury

Impressionist Palette: Quilt Color & Design, Gai Perry

Impressionist Quilts, Gai Perry

Kaleidoscopes & Quilts, Paula Nadelstern

Laurel Burch Quilts: Kindred Creatures, Laurel Burch

Lone Star Quilts and Beyond: Step-by-Step Projects and Inspiration, Jan Krentz

Make Any Block Any Size: Easy Drawing Method, Unlimited Pattern Possibilities, Sensational Quilt Designs, Joen Wolfrom

Patchwork Persuasion: Fascinating Quilts from Traditional Designs, Joen Wolfrom

Photo Transfer Handbook, The: Snap It, Print It, Stitch It!, Jean Ray Laury

Pieced Flowers, Ruth B. McDowell

Pieced Vegetables, Ruth B. McDowell

Piecing: Expanding the Basics, Ruth B. McDowell

Provence Quilts and Cuisine, Marie-Christine Flocard & Cosabeth Parriaud

Q is for Quilt, Diana McClun & Laura Nownes

Quilted Garden, The: Design & Make Nature-Inspired Quilts, Jane Sassaman

Quilting Back to Front: Fun & Easy No-Mark Techniques, Larraine Scouler

Quilting with Carol Armstrong: •*30 Quilting Patterns*•*Appliqué Designs*•*16 Projects*, Carol Armstrong

Quilts for Guys: 15 Fun Projects For Your Favorite Fella, Compilation

Quilts from the Civil War: Nine Projects, Historic Notes, Diary Entries, Barbara Brackman

Ultimate Guide to Longarm Quilting, The: •*How to Use Any Longarm Machine* •*Techniques, Patterns & Pantographs* •*Starting a Business* •*Hiring a Longarm Machine Quilter*, Linda Taylor

Rag Wool Appliqué: •*Easy to Sew* •*Use Any Sewing Machine* •*Quilts, Home Decor & Clothing*, Kathy MacMannis

Scrap Quilts: The Art of Making Do, Roberta Horton

Setting Solutions, Sharyn Craig

Shadow Quilts, Patricia Magaret & Donna Slusser

Skydyes: A Visual Guide to Fabric Painting, Mickey Lawler

Smashing Sets: Exciting Ways to Arrange Quilt Blocks, Margaret J. Miller

Strips 'n Curves: A New Spin on Strip Piecing, Louisa L. Smith

Through the Garden Gate: Quilters and Their Gardens, Jean & Valori Wells

Tradition with a Twist: Variations on Your Favorite Quilts, Blanche Young & Dalene Young-Stone

Wild Birds: Designs for Appliqué & Quilting, Carol Armstrong

Wildflowers: Designs for Appliqué and Quilting, Carol Armstrong

Workshop with Velda Newman, A: Adding Dimension to Your Quilts, Velda E. Newman

For more information write
for a free catalog:
C&T Publishing, Inc.
P.O. Box 1456
Lafayette, CA 94549
(800) 284-1114
e-mail: ctinfo@ctpub.com
website:www.ctpub.com

For quilting supplies:
Cotton Patch Mail Order
3405 Hall Lane, Dept. CTB
Lafayette, CA 94549
(800) 835-4418
(925) 283-7883
e-mail: quiltusa@yahoo.com
website: www.quiltusa.com